12 95

The
ELAN VALLEY
CLEARANCE

Elan Valley Junction of Rivers Elan and Claerwen

The junction of the Elan and Claerwen rivers which would eventually provide the city of Birmingham with its new water supply. Nant-Gwyllt House, home to the Lewis Lloyd family, can be seen in the centre with its lodge to the right (*date unknown, but probably 1890s*)

The

ELAN VALLEY
CLEARANCE

*The Fate of the People & Places affected by
the 1892 Elan Valley Reservoir Scheme*

DAVID LEWIS BROWN

LOGASTON PRESS

First published in 2019, reprinted 2020 by Logaston Press
The Holme, Church Road, Eardisley HR3 6NJ
www.logastonpress.co.uk
An imprint of Fircone Books Ltd.

ISBN 978-1-910839-36-2

Designed and typeset by Richard Wheeler.
Cover design by Richard Wheeler.

Printed and bound in Poland

Logaston Press is committed to a sustainable future for our business, our readers and our planet. The book in your hands is made from paper certified by the Forest Stewardship Council.

British Library Catalogue in Publishing Data.
A CIP catalogue record for this book is available from the British Library.

CONTENTS

ACKNOWLEDGEMENTS

Firstly, I would like to mention Hazel Jones, my aunt, sadly no longer with us. She used to talk to me about the Elan Valley and encouraged my interest, and without her this project would never have happened. I would also like to thank Richard and Gill Hughes, Betty Davies and Lloyd Lewis for their local knowledge and for allowing me to use some of their photographs; and Pastor Ronald Downey for allowing me access to the Elan Valley Bethania Baptist Chapel records. I am indebted to the staff of Powys County Archives in Llandrindod Wells for all their wonderful help and assistance in my research. Thanks also go to the Elan Valley Trust, the National Museum of Wales, the Library of Birmingham and the Hergest Trust Archive. I would like to thank Richard and Su Wheeler of Logaston Press for all their suggestions and ideas for improving the book, for pulling my original manuscript into shape and for making it all possible. Along with that thanks must also go to Daisy Powell for suggesting I get in touch with Logaston Press. Last but by no means least, I must say thank you to my friends and family for their assistance and support.

Hazel and her brother Glyn by the Gareg-ddu viaduct, with Nant-Gwyllt Church in the background

In Memory of Dorothy Hazel Jones, 1930–2017

PREFACE

Today, the Elan Valley is a renowned tourist attraction a few miles from the town of Rhayader in Mid Wales, visited by thousands of people each year. But 130 years ago it was very different. The valleys of the Elan and Claerwen rivers were remote places, little known to those outside the area. This would all change when the area was chosen as the place to provide the city of Birmingham, some 70 miles away to the east, with a new water supply.

Although I was not born in Wales my ancestry is deeply rooted in the Rhayader area, due to the building of the Elan Valley dams and reservoirs at the turn of the twentieth century. My great-grandfather, John Brown, brought his family from Oswestry in Shropshire to the valley where he found work labouring on the vast scheme. When the dams were complete he returned to Shropshire along with his wife and two daughters. However, his two sons – John (my grandfather) and his brother Richard – stayed on in the area and found work on various farms. They married local girls and both made their homes in Rhayader. My father Glyn Brown was born in Rhayader and worked on the later Claerwen scheme before moving away. I also had an uncle (Howard Evans the blacksmith) who worked on the Claerwen scheme and remained as part of the workforce maintaining the dams; and an aunt (Hazel Price/ Jones née Brown) who also worked on the Claerwen scheme before spending the majority of her working life in the Elan Estate Office. Members of my family still live in and around Rhayader today.

I have known the valleys of the Elan and Claerwen since childhood when, as a family, we would come on our annual summer holiday to stay with my grandparents, John and Sarah Brown at Oakfield House in Rhayader. As I grew older I became fascinated in what the valleys would have looked like before the dams were built, and since retiring I have done a great deal of research looking into this.

Much has been written on the construction of the dams, and I will touch on this too, but this book will concentrate mainly on the effects the scheme had on the people and places of the valleys, covering the period 1891 to 1911 – a sort of 'before and after'. My research is based on the original 1892 scheme, which also included the plan to build three dams on the River Claerwen at a later date. Due to the passage of time and the improvements in technology these three dams were never completed, and instead were replaced with just one, namely the Claerwen dam.

Using census returns, electoral rolls, parish registers, old photographs, documents, newspapers, books and maps, I will try to describe a journey through the valley before the construction work began, and tell the story of the places lost and what happened to the people and their families destined to be displaced by the building of the dams and reservoirs. It will be a mixture of local history, social history and family history.

So, when you next make a visit to the Elan Valley and marvel at the great feat of engineering in the building of the dams, take a while to transport yourself back to a time before it all began.

All royalties received from the sale of this book will be donated to various charities

PART 1
A Journey through the Valleys of the Elan & Claerwen

☞

Detail of Terrier Plan "O", by surveyor Stephen Williams, 1893, tracing the path of the River Elan as it heads south and joins with the River Claerwen, showing a number of properties within the watershed, some of which would eventually be lost to the Caban-coch reservoir, including Nant-Gwyllt

I T's April 1891, and over the next few years the valleys of the Elan and Claerwen will change forever as the building of dams and reservoirs to provide Birmingham with a water supply gets underway. The effects on the people and places of the valleys will be great, the landscape will change, many places will be lost to flooding or abandoned, and many of the people will be scattered far and wide.

Using old maps and other contemporary sources, let me take you on a journey through the two valleys on the eve of this great disturbance. The area covered on this journey will go from Pont-ar-Elan, then follow the Elan downstream to the point where the Caban-coch dam stands today (*see 'D' on plan, p. 5*) and then we will retrace our steps to the junction of the Elan and Claerwen rivers where we will then follow the Claerwen upstream as far as Claerwen farm (**67**).

Our starting point: Pont-ar-Elan (date unknown, but probably 1890s). The bridge over the river can be seen at the bottom left (*Richard Hughes Collection*)

List of Place Names

Spellings and formation of names are taken from the 1st edition Ordnance Survey maps 1891

1. Lluest-Torclawdd
2. Lluest-cwm-bach
3. Hirnant
4. Aber-Calettwr
5. Lluest-aber-caethon
6. Lluest-calettwr
7. Llanerch-lleyn
8. Ty-nant
9. Troed-rhiw-drain
10. Allt-goch-fach
11. Allt-goch
12. Pen-y-gareg
13. Pen-y-bont
14. Dol-faenog
15. Ty'n-y-llidiart
16. Dol-folau
17. Cringwm
18. Ty'n-y-ffald
19. Llanerch-ty-newydd
20. Cwm-Elan House
21. Cwm-Elan Mine
22. Cwm-Elan Lodge
23. Henfron
24. Cwm-Coel

25. Blaen-Coel
26. Baptist Chapel & cottage
27. Gareg-ddu
28. Shop-bach
29. Pen-henbren
30. Llanerchi
31. Glan-yr-afon
32. Nant-Gwyllt School
33. Nant-Gwyllt Church
34. Ty-bach
35. Tan-y-foel
36. Abernant
37. Gro Mill
38. Gro-isaf
39. Gro-bach
40. Nant-Gwyllt Cottage (1)
41. Nant-Gwyllt Cottage (2)
42. Nant-Gwyllt Lodge
43. Gro-uchaf
44. Nant-Gwyllt House
45. Pant-y-blodau

46. Pen-glan-Einon
47. Pen-cae-haidd
48. Pant-tawel
49. Dol-y-mynach
50. Marchnant
51. Pen-rhiwlan
52. Llanerch-y-cawr
53. Ty'n-y-gors
54. Llwyn-dale
55. Dalrhiw
56. Nant-y-Carw Mine
57. Rhiwnant
58. Pen-y-gwaith
59. Cwm-clyd
60. Nant-y-Car
61. Bryn-Iago
62. Cil-oerwynt
63. Cerig-cwplau
64. Lluest-y-gader
65. Nant-y-beddau
66. Pant-y-beddau
67. Claerwen Farm

THE ELAN & CLAERWEN VALLEYS
Showing the locations of the properties and the dams

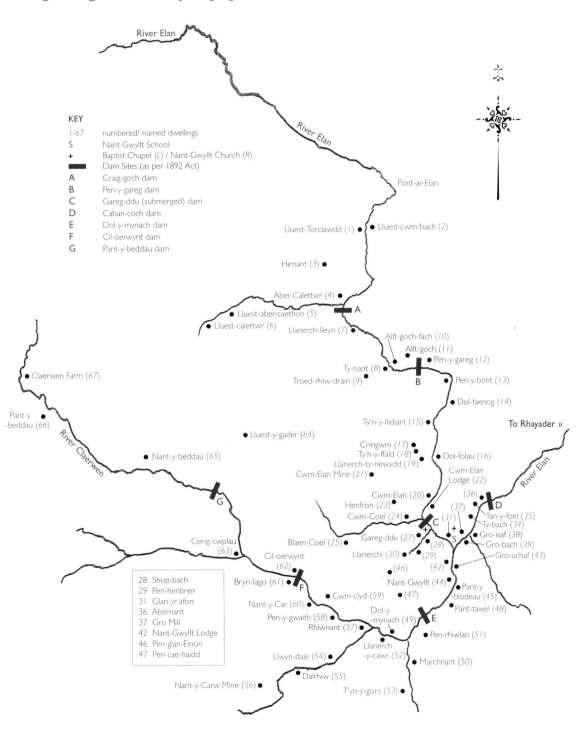

River Elan

River Elan

River Elan

River Claerwen

To Rhayader »

Pont-ar-Elan

KEY

1-67	numbered/ named dwellings
S	Nant-Gwyllt School
+	Baptist Chapel (*L*) / Nant-Gwyllt Church (*R*)
▬	Dam Sites (as per 1892 Act)
A	Craig-goch dam
B	Pen-y-gareg dam
C	Gareg-ddu (submerged) dam
D	Caban-coch dam
E	Dol-y-mynach dam
F	Cil-oerwynt dam
G	Pant-y-beddau dam

Lluest-Torclawdd (*1*)
Lluest-cwm-bach (*2*)
Hirnant (*3*)
Aber-Calettwr (*4*) A
Lluest-aber-caethon (*5*)
Lluest-calettwr (*6*)
Llanerch-lleyn (*7*)
Allt-goch-fach (*10*)
Allt-goch (*11*)
Pen-y-gareg (*12*)
Ty-nant (*8*)
Troed-rhiw-drain (*9*) B
Pen-y-bont (*13*)
Claerwen Farm (*67*)
Dol-faenog (*14*)
Ty'n-y-llidiart (*15*)
Pant-y-beddau (*66*)
Lluest-y-gader (*64*)
Cringwm (*17*)
Ty'n-y-ffald (*18*)
Dol-folau (*16*)
Llanerch-ty-newydd (*19*)
Cwm-Elan Mine (*21*)
Nant-y-beddau (*65*)
Cwm-Elan Lodge (*22*)
Cwm-Elan (*20*)
(*36*) D
Henfron (*23*)
(*37*) Tan-y-foel (*35*)
Ty-bach (*34*)
G
Cwm-Coel (*24*)
(*31*) C
Gareg-ddu (*27*) + S
Gro-isaf (*38*)
Gro-bach (*39*)
Cerig-cwplau (*63*)
Blaen-Coel (*25*)
Llanerchi (*30*)
(*28*)
(*29*) Gro-uchaf (*43*)
Cil-oerwynt (*62*)
(*46*) (*42*)
Bryn-Iago (*61*)
Nant-Gwyllt (*44*) Pant-y-blodeau (*45*)
F
Cwm-clyd (*59*)
(*47*)
Pant-tawel (*48*)
Nant-y-Car (*60*)
Pen-y-gwaith (*58*)
Dol-y-mynach (*49*) E
Rhiwnant (*57*)
Pen-rhiwlan (*51*)
Llwyn-dale (*54*)
Llanerch-y-cawr (*52*)
Marchnant (*50*)
Dalrhiw (*55*)
Nant-y-Carw Mine (*56*)
Tyn-y-gors (*53*)

28	Shop-bach
29	Pen-henbren
31	Glan-yr-afon
36	Abernant
37	Gro Mill
42	Nant-Gwyllt Lodge
46	Pen-glan-Einon
47	Pen-cae-haidd

The snows of last month have gone and hopefully spring is on its way. We start our journey at Pont-ar-Elan, the small bridge over the river about five miles from Rhayader, just off the old turnpike road which leads to Aberystwyth. As we stand on the bridge, at around 1,000 feet above sea level, looking west, below us a dipper bobs up and down on the rocks, and we see the River Elan meandering away from us to its source around five miles away on the borders of Cardiganshire. We will follow the river in the opposite direction.

At first our route goes straight on, taking to the rising ground, cutting off the loop in the river, but in no time it descends to where the river has widened and the track fords through it. We are on the right-hand bank of the river, travelling downstream. Our track now hugs the riverside and we are surrounded by moorland sheepwalks rising to around 1,500 feet, the grasses still showing the browns and yellows of winter. The lambing season will soon be under way, with many of the ewes in the sheepfolds or sheltered ground, to give birth to their new lambs. After about a mile, a track goes off to our right and we can see a small farmstead just along the track. This is Lluest-Torclawdd (1) situated on the Esgair Rhiw Elan sheepwalk. Further along this track and just out of sight is the Hirnant farm (3). If we now turn round and look to our left over to the opposite side of the river, on the hill facing us is Lluest-cwm-bach (2), a shepherd's cottage situated on the Newhouse sheepwalk. Continuing on our riverside

Looking back at the route we have taken so far, and at the site of Craig-goch dam
(*Richard Hughes Collection*)

track, crossing the Nant Torclawdd stream on its way to join the Elan, the track soon begins to climb up and away from the river, and we look down on the river making its way through a rocky, boulder-strewn section, on the other side of which we can see a small sheepfold. The distinct sound of the curlew fills the air as we pass by another sheepfold close to the right of the track, before making our way around some rocks then dropping down to the property of Aber-Calettwr (4), a whitewashed cottage like so many others in the valley. It is so-named as it is situated at the mouth of the Calettwr stream which flows into the Elan. A track leads up behind Aber-Calettwr and follows the stream. If we were to take this, in about a mile we would reach Lluest-aber-caethon (5), and a little further up the track is Lluest-calettwr (6). Instead we ford across the Calettwr stream and climb away from Aber-Calettwr. As we ascend, the river makes a left-hand turn, the valley narrows and we have rocky hills rising above us on both sides; our path reaches 1,100 feet and we see below us the river racing through a narrow rocky gorge. It is at this point that the uppermost dam of the Birmingham scheme will be built.

We continue on the higher ground above the river, and shortly cross the Nant Gris stream as it flows down from the hills. The valley now begins to open up again on our side to more open moorland, with the river keeping close to the craggy slopes of Craig yr Allt-goch opposite. The track then starts to descend past Llanerch-lleyn (7) back

Looking back from Ty-nant towards the site of the Craig-goch dam. The small cottage in the right of the picture is Allt-goch-fach amid a patchwork of fields and backed by Craig yr Allt-goch
(*Richard Hughes Collection*)

towards the river. The landscape has changed here, and the lower slopes opposite have become clothed in woodland, and the valley bottom a patchwork of small fields and hay meadows, dotted with a mixture of trees. We are passing through these fields, and on a short length of the track bordered by trees as we approach Ty-nant (8). By the time we reach here we are back down to around 1,000 feet. A track leads down from Ty-nant to the river and crosses a wooden bridge to Allt-goch-fach (10). Up above Ty-nant, behind us and out of sight, is the farm of Troed-rhiw-drain (9).

From Ty-nant our route crosses the Nant Brithgwm stream by a ford and then turns sharp left, as does the river at this point. Once again the two sides of the valley begin to narrow. On the opposite side of the river below the wooded slopes we see the farm of Allt-goch (11). The track is now descending, the riverside fields have disappeared, the river bed has become rocky, forming rapids, and we are surrounded by high ground on three sides. Opposite us on the rising hill is Pen-y-gareg farm (12). Behind us is the high moor of Gwaelod y Rhos, and in front of us rises the craggy slopes of Craig Dol-faenog – all these rising to well over 1,500 feet. These last two farms, Allt-goch and Pen-y-gareg, have been the homes of the Hughes and Evans families for generations. We now drop down to the river, to where it is forced through a long, narrow, rocky gorge forming waterfalls and torrents as it goes. We cross the river by a precarious single-plank bridge known as Pont Hyllfan, meaning 'ugly bridge', almost not daring to look down into the deep, black hole below us. We are down at around 800 feet now, and it is just upstream of this point that the Birmingham Corporation will build another dam.

Now on the left bank of the river, our way climbs a little and goes up through a few trees, with the river below us just emerging from the rocky channel. We follow the river as it bends round to the right, and in the curve of the river on the opposite bank stands Pen-y-bont (13). We descend a little and by the time we reach Dol-faenog (14) we are back down at 800 feet. This property sits just by the riverside and is situated in the thin strip of land between the river and the backdrop of Craig Dol-faenog above us, which in the summer will be a mass of heather, gorse and whinberries. The fields stretch along the valley bottom on both sides of the river – those on the other side reached by a ford and stepping stones. Opposite Dol-faenog the slopes are dotted with rocks lower down and with sheepwalks above. We climb a little here as we follow the path which borders the fields and we continue our journey downstream. The valley begins to widen even more and we can see up ahead, on the opposite side of the river, the property of Ty'n-y-lliadiart farm (15) situated amongst fields backed by sheepwalks. Once opposite Ty'n-y-lliadiart we begin to climb away from the river, which again at this point narrows and is forced through the rocky bed. The mewing of a buzzard can be heard as it soars above us. Next we enter some woodland and ford across the Nant Dol-folau stream as it tumbles down the hillside and joins the Elan. The river is now further away from us, as more fields border the river on our side. A little further along our way, we come to the farm of Dol-folau (16) nestled amongst

Photograph taken in 1895 from a point just above, and upstream from, where we crossed
Pont Hyllfan, with some of the railway already in place. From this viewpoint we are looking
back to where we have just been, and at the site of Pen-y-gareg dam
(*by permission of the Powys Archives R/X/241/1/15*)

trees, below Dol-folau rocks some 200 feet above us where the *kronk-kronk* of ravens
can be heard. On the hill opposite, which is now wooded on its lower slopes, are
three properties: Cringwm (17), Ty'n-y-ffald (18) and Llanerch-ty-newydd (19) situated amongst fields above the trees.

   As we continue our journey along the paths which border the fields around Dol-
folau, in about half a mile on the other side of the river the stables and farm buildings
of Cwm-Elan come into view, and behind them a densely-wooded hill with oaks and
pines rises to 1,400 feet. Above us, on our side, is a strip of woodland bordering the
fields. This soon widens to cover our track, and although the trees are not yet in leaf
they are a mixture of oak, beech, birch and alder, and among them the small birds
are busy singing and preparing for the nesting season. In a short while we arrive at
the gateway which would take us over the stone humpback bridge across the river
and along the entrance road bordered by trees to Cwm-Elan House (20) which can
be seen from this point across a wide expanse of grassland with a backdrop of trees.

Photograph taken in 1895, looking upstream from the area around Dol-folau
(*by permission of the Library of Birmingham MS944/114/15*)

The approach to Cwm-Elan House over the humpback bridge (*Richard Hughes Collection*)

Also around the house are gardens, greenhouses and tennis courts. Thomas Grove purchased the Cwm-Elan estate in 1792, improved it and turned it into his summer residence. Since being sold by the Grove family, it has passed through many hands to the present owner, Robert Lewis Lloyd. The house is described by A.G. Bradley (who made his visit during the time of the construction of the dams) in his book *Highways and Byways in South Wales* as, 'A plain four-storied house with lofty wings, nestling at the foot of an almost perpendicular hill, thickly clad to its summit with pines and hemlocks and oaks. Strips of smooth meadow-land lie between the garden and the Elan, which courses between woody banks down the narrow vale'. Living in the house at this time, along with some staff, are three civil engineers – a sign of things to come.

High above the house, in the valley of the Nant Methan stream, is Cwm-Elan Mine (21) which is no longer worked and has been abandoned. Back on our side of the river we continue and soon pass Cwm-Elan Lodge (22). Opposite here, high on the hill, is the Henfron farm (23) surrounded by fields. Shortly after passing the lodge, the river begins to make a sharp left-hand turn, and at this point, on the opposite side of the river flowing down to meet the Elan, is the stream of Cwm-Coel. If we look across the stream we see the farm of the same name (24), and if we were to follow the stream further it would lead us up to Blaen-Coel (25).

After this point the valley begins to narrow and the path comes closer to the river once more as we make our way between the wooded slopes of Coed-y-foel on our side and the wooded slopes of Coed Aber-Elan on the other. We are now approaching the heart of the valley, close to the junction of the two rivers. Clustered around here are a number of properties, including a church, chapel and school. We soon reach a footbridge over the river, situated over a waterfall. It is roughly at this point that the Birmingham Corporation will build another dam (this time a submerged one, with a viaduct carrying a road across the reservoir). Before we continue on our path we will cross the bridge, turn left and soon arrive at the Baptist Chapel (26) with its graveyard of lichen-covered stones, and adjacent whitewashed cottage. Just behind the chapel a tree-lined track climbs the hill, following the course of a stream which comes down to join the Elan. The first property we see, on the right of the track, is Gareg-ddu (27) with its garden around it. Next, but now on the left-hand side of the track and stream, is the two-roomed cottage, Shop-bach (28), home to 80-year-old Anne Griffiths, who has lived there for many years. Above that is Pen-henbren (29), and further up towards the top of the hill stands Llanerchi farm (30).

If we now retrace our steps back across the bridge, turning right and continuing on our way, we pass a river crossing of stepping stones, and then we come to Glan-yr-afon (31) almost hidden in the trees. The track continues around the wooded slopes and starts to turn to the left, away from the river, and the valley floor once again opens up into a wide patchwork of fields which, as the seasons turn, will produce hay and other crops such as oats and barley. In a short distance we reach Nant-Gwyllt School (32) with its

Nant-Gwyllt School

Birmingham Corporation offices

A picture taken shortly after work had begun, looking back from where we have just been, and roughly from Nant-Gwyllt cottages (by permission of Powys Archives R/D/CL/1/23)

NANTGWILLT VALLEY.

Nant-Gwyllt Church

Site of the Caban-coch dam

house and playground. This dates back to 1869 when it was leased to Miss Margaret Gertrude Lewis Lloyd, a sister to Robert Lewis Lloyd. Today it is being run by school mistress Elizabeth Abley, assisted by her sister Alice. A little further on we come to Nant-Gwyllt Church (33), built in 1772 by Thomas Lewis Lloyd as a chapel of ease. A lane leads down to the right from here, which we will return to shortly. The road from here improves, as this is the main road from Rhayader to Nant-Gwyllt, and our journey continues below the rocky, scree-covered slopes of Craig-y-foel. We soon come to the small cottage of Ty-bach (34), then a short distance on another cottage, Tan-y-foel (35) sheltered by scots pines, home to Benjamin Davies and his family (Benjamin and his son are both tailors). Across the road from here is Abernant cottage (36), home to the Baptist Minister, Seth Thomas, who also runs a small shop here. Just after this the valley reaches its lowest and narrowest point, at about 720 feet, and squeezes between the steep, rocky hills on either side, with Craig Gigfran on the left and Craig Cnwch on the right rising to 1,300 feet. Here, the Birmingham Corporation will build the Caban-coch dam, the last on the River Elan.

We have travelled roughly seven miles since we started out from Pont-ar-Elan, and we now turn around. Retracing our steps back past the cottages of Abernant, Tan-y-foel and Ty-bach, once again we arrive at Nant-Gwyllt Church in its fenced enclosure surrounded by trees, with its ivy and moss-covered, whitewashed walls. Here, we follow the lane to the left, which takes us across the valley floor back towards the Elan. First, we pass Gro Mill (37), a water-powered mill which has been lived in, and run by, the Lloyd family for generations, and is now in the hands of John Lloyd and his family, some of whom work as carpenters. The valley community bring their crops here for grinding and their timber for sawing; there is also a kiln house for drying grain.

Opposite the mill is another lane which leads back to the school, but we continue along our way, the lane bordered on both sides with hedges and trees. As we come closer to the river we can see, on the hill opposite, the Nant-y-gro stream flowing down on its way to join the Elan. On either side of the stream, backed by the wooded hill, are the farms of Gro-isaf (38) and Gro-bach (39). Our road turns right and is now almost parallel to the river, leading us all the way to a bridge where we cross the Elan, the bridge situated just above its junction with the River Claerwen. After crossing the bridge we come to Nant-Gwyllt Cottages (40–41). These are sometimes referred to as 'new cottages' as they were built to house staff employed by the Lewis Lloyd family at Nant-Gwyllt House. Today one of the cottages is shared by a gardener and a coachman, but the other one is the home of Anne Conway and her family, her husband at present living at Dalrhiw in the Rhiwnant valley where he has resided and made his living mining copper and lead for over 25 years.

Our way now turns left and we soon come to Nant-Gwyllt Lodge (42) situated right by the junction of the two rivers, and home to a gamekeeper in the employ of the Lewis Lloyd family.

So, from now on our journey follows the River Claerwen upstream on its right-hand bank. From the lodge, we pass lawn tennis courts and a summerhouse, all backed by the wooded hillside of Coed Gelynen. At this point, on the opposite side of the river, stands the farm Gro-uchaf (43) which can be reached by a ford. Soon after, we arrive at the entrance to Nant-Gwyllt House (44). This is home to the Lewis Lloyd family, the major landowners in the valley, together with a number of servants. As well as the house, with its steps onto a lawn that leads down to the river, there is a coach house, stables, kennels, greenhouses, ponds, shrubbery, walled gardens, pleasure grounds with ornamental trees and a farm with its associated buildings. The house is believed to date from the sixteenth century, and is described in *Cassell's Family Magazine* of 1893 as:

> a large home-like-looking house built in a lovely nook on the side of a hill. Within a stone's throw of the windows the river rushes along its rocky bed, fir-trees and oaks bend over the water, and on every side are the beautiful hills, purple, grey and golden brown. A high wall of moss-grown grey stone runs round the house and grounds, and inside are the stables, farm-buildings, carpenters' and gardeners' cottages, a perfect little colony, busy and happy within it's own area.

Richard Eustace Tickell, one of the civil engineers now residing at Cwm-Elan House, described it in his book, *The Vale of Nantgwilt*, written in 1894, as 'romantically situated on a projecting spur, in the midst of magnificent fir trees, backed by the shady glen which gives its name to the house; a lawn in front slopes down to the river, affording a fine view down the broad vale to the eastward.'

On the opposite bank of the river, across from Nant-Gwyllt House, is the cottage Pant-y-blodau (45), home to Evan Jones. Evan farms Nant-Gwyllt farm, which he accesses by a footbridge over the river. High above and behind Nant-Gwyllt House stands Pen-glan-Einon (46).

Our route now passes behind the house. The surface of the road becomes poorer once again and we continue through the woodland, gradually descending to 800 feet and back down to the riverside. Above us here, at well over 1,300 feet, stands Pen-cae-haidd (47), and across the river from us is the small cottage of Pan-tawel (48). Soon we come to a fork in the track: it is at this point that the Birmingham Corporation will build another dam. The right-hand fork of the track takes you to the farm of Dol-y-mynach (49), but we stay on the riverside path and emerge from the woodland into the meadows that border the river, and make our way to a wooden bridge. If we look behind us across the meadows, we can now see the farm of Dol-y-mynach. It is a very large, grand old house and untypical of a valley farmhouse, its appearance suggesting it is of much higher status. It is said that it was connected with the monks of Strata Florida, who once owned all this land – and indeed its name means 'monks meadow', which presumably refers to the meadow we are looking across. The backdrop to the house is the hill of Craig-y-Mynach, meaning 'monks crag'.

As we cross the bridge, below us is a lone fisherman trying his luck for a trout early in the season. Also, by crossing this bridge we are leaving Radnorshire and entering Breconshire, the river forming the county boundary, and we cross from the parish of Cwmdeuddwr into the parish of Llanwrthwl. Looking left here the Marchnant stream comes down to enter the river. Up above is the farm of Marchnant (50), and further along to the left is Pen-rhiwlan (51). Our way turns right from the bridge and follows the river with fields to the left of us, and we soon reach Llanerch-y-cawr (52) a little above the river. This is a typical Welsh longhouse, said to date from the 1500s, and a former Baptist meeting house. It is now home to Evan Stephens and his family, whose ancestors have lived here for 50 years or more. In this type of farmhouse the family live at one end and the animals at the opposite end. Up above here, paths climb to Ty'n-y-gors (53). We continue along a lane now lined with hedges of hawthorn and blackthorn. A track leads off to the left, and if we took this it would lead us up into the Rhiwnant valley and to the properties of Llwyn-dale (54) and Dalrhiw (55) (both of these being miner's cottages) and then onto Nant-y-Carw Mine.

We carry on along the lane, briefly returning to the riverside before the lane (now with dry-stone walling on one side), branches left across meadows before reaching a bridge and ford over the River Rhiwnant. Soon after crossing the bridge we reach the Rhiwnant farm (57). Passing through here, the stony track now begins to climb and we soon reach almost 1,000 feet and a junction of pathways joining the main track. Situated here is the old miner's cottage of Pen-y-gwaith (58), the hills here dotted with old mine shafts. We are high above the river, and down below us we can hear and see the River Claerwen rushing through big boulders forming a large cataract. Continuing along the main track once again we are gradually descending and heading for the river bank. On the way, across the valley is the farm of Cwm-clyd (59), and when we reach the river we are right next to Nant-y-Car (60) situated in the bend of the river, surrounded by some fields and a meadow facing the farm but on the opposite bank, accessed by fording the river.

The path skirts around the farm, following the curve of the river, and we are now travelling parallel to the river, a little above it. The valley has narrowed and on both sides of us the hills are dotted with trees and their tops covered with rocky crags. Shortly, we see below us a rocky cleft with the river forced through forming a waterfall, and just after this the river turns left and our path follows it. At this point another dam is planned. Just around the bend in the path, below us and near to the river bank is Bryn-Iago (61) and directly across the river from here is Cil-oerwynt farm (62), another Welsh longhouse. Our path continues close to the river, with rocky hills to our right and the Nant-y-Car sheepwalk above us to our left. After about a mile we ford the Arban river and arrive at the shepherd's cottage of Cerig-cwplau (63) sitting at the foot of a rocky crag and surrounded by a distinctive low stone enclosure.

A picture taken from behind Nant-Gwyllt House in 1892
(by permission of the Library of Birmingham MS944 BCC ST 2008/214/Box 45)

We have travelled around five miles from Nant-Gwyllt, and from now on the valley opens up and becomes even more remote, the landscape changing to that of moorland – just like the terrain on which we started this journey. The Claerwen river winds its way through the valley, and our track proceeds across the hillside, a little above the river, crossing various sheepwalks belonging to different farms. After just less than a mile, on the opposite side of the river, we see the Nant-y-gader stream entering the Claerwen. A track follows this stream and leads to another shepherd's cottage: that of Lluest-y-gader (**64**). Just upriver from where the stream enters, our track squeezes between rocks on both sides and we come nearer to the riverside. This is where the Birmingham Corporation's final dam on the Claerwen is planned.

The track now continues, and in a short distance comes down to meet the river's edge where we ford across back into Radnorshire. Turning left we climb a little, ford another stream and follow the path over the hillside, soon passing a track leading off to our right, which if taken would bring us to Nant-y-beddau farm (**65**). After fording another stream, looking to our left over into Breconshire, amongst the hills in the distance over a mile away, is Pant-y-beddau (**66**). In about another two miles, after fording a couple more streams, our track reaches the end of our journey at Claerwen

Farm (67). After starting our journey at Pont-ar-Elan at about 1,000 feet we have descended to around 700 feet at the point where the Caban-coch dam is planned; and now, outside Claerwen Farm, we have risen to 1,300 feet with some of the hills around us reaching 1,700 feet. This remote spot is home to Thomas Lewis who has lived here and shepherded on the hills for over 50 years, along with his family. Being close to the Cardiganshire border they speak only Welsh, like many of their neighbours who are sparsely dotted amongst these hills.

The journey through the valleys of the Elan and Claerwen has covered an area in which there are 65 places of habitation (only 56 being occupied at that time) together with a church, chapel and school, as listed at the time of the 1891 census, which records 287 people living in the two valleys.

Of the people living in the two valleys the majority spoke both English and Welsh, with around 100 speaking just English and about 30 speaking only Welsh.

Many of the tracks taken on our journey can still be followed today (*see Part 6, p. 151*), and when you visit the Elan Valley you may come across the ruins of some of the old cottages and farmhouses. If you do, take a moment to think about the people who were about to lose their homes and livelihoods.

PLAN

shewing

MANOR BOUNDARIES

AND

MANORIAL RIGHTS

acquired by the

Corporation of Birmingham.

BLAEN-Y-CWM
PEN-Y-BRYN

TY-MAWR

CROWN MANOR of MEVENITH
(LOWER GWNNWS PARISH)
Minerals only acquired.

PART 2

Why the Elan & Claerwen Valleys?

The Birmingham Corporation Water Act 1892

☞

Detail of Manor Boundaries Plan, by surveyor John Jones, 1893 or 1894

2

A S EARLY AS 1870 the Elan and Claerwen valleys were being looked at for the supply of water for Birmingham. Following an unfavourable report, the Birmingham Corporation knew that it wouldn't be too long before the supply of water to the city became inadequate. The Corporation asked Robert Rawlinson, a Government Inspector, to produce a report on where future supplies might be obtained. Rawlinson then engaged the civil engineers James Mansergh and John Lawson, and after considering various alternatives the pair recommended the valleys of the Elan and Claerwen. In 1871, Rawlinson in turn proposed this solution to the Birmingham Corporation. At this time the town's water supply was under the control of the Birmingham Waterworks Company. The Corporation had made various attempts to gain control of the waterworks, but it was not until the passing of the Birmingham Corporation Water Act 1875 that this was granted. After this the Corporation continued to gain further supplies from their existing local sources. However, by 1890, and with demand growing from a fast-rising population, increased industrialisation and the effects from pollution and outbreaks of disease, it became a matter of urgency that a new source of good, clean water be found that could supply the city for the next 25–50 years.

In 1891 the population of the area being supplied with water by the Birmingham Corporation was over 600,000 people, and in his plans Mr Mansergh had estimated that the number of consumers would increase at the rate of 3% per year over the next ten years. This would mean that demand would increase from just over 15 million gallons per day to over 20 million gallons during this period.

The Water Committee requested that J.W. Gray, engineer of the Water Department, and James Mansergh report on what could be done to provide a sufficient water supply for Birmingham. A detailed investigation was undertaken into the local supply, but it was deemed that local sources could not be relied upon to provide the quality and quantity of water required. The search would need to look further afield, the main criteria required set out as follows:

1. HIGH QUALITY OF WATER
2. SUFFICIENT QUANTITY TO PROVIDE WATER FOR AT LEAST 50 YEARS
3. THE ABILITY FOR THE WATER TO BE FED TO BIRMINGHAM BY GRAVITY

Messrs Gray and Mansergh looked south and east; then to the north where the rivers Derwent and Trent were considered, but discounted in terms of quality. Next, the search headed westwards, where the rivers Severn, Teme, Ithon and Wye came under consideration, before the pair finally settled on the rivers of the Elan and Claerwen – James Mansergh's original choice. The water here met all of the Corporation's requirements in terms of quality, quantity and elevation to allow delivery by gravity.

In 1891, James Mansergh's report recommending the scheme was presented to the Birmingham Corporation, and these plans, which would form the basis of the subsequent Act of Parliament, were approved by the Water Committee. Late in 1891, notice was given by the Birmingham Corporation that an application for a Bill was to be put before the next session of Parliament. The aim of the Bill was to create an Act to allow the Corporation to construct the dams and reservoirs necessary to capture the waters of the Elan and Claerwen valleys, in order to provide a new water supply for the city of Birmingham.

The Bill's Progress through Parliament

Unsurprisingly perhaps, there was much opposition to the Birmingham Corporation's plans – not just from the locality where the works would take place but also from London and South Wales where there was unhappiness that Birmingham was trying to claim a water supply which they themselves may want to draw upon in the future; and there were people against it even in Birmingham itself, mainly on financial grounds.

After a first reading in February 1892, the Bill came to Parliament for its second reading on 8 March 1892. In a debate lasting more than three hours, many points were raised, both for and against the Bill, by various Members of Parliament. A number of points raised in this debate are worth looking at in some detail, for the light they shed on how the Bill was to affect the people of the two valleys and surrounding district. At the heart of much of the debate were exchanges centring on the rights of those who lived and worked in the valleys, whose lives and livelihoods would be directly impacted upon by the works.

The Bill was promoted in Parliament by Mr Joseph Chamberlain, the MP for Birmingham West; and opposed by, amongst others, Mr Thomas Ellis, the MP for Merionethshire. Mr Ellis wanted the rights of commoners and others protected. Mr Chamberlain stated that, 'the Corporation of Birmingham do not desire to interfere in the slightest degree with any rights that can be shown to exist on the part of commoners or others, except so far as to secure the purity of the water supply.' He went on to point out the practices that could adversely affect this were the cutting of turf and sheep washing.

In the course of the debate, Mr Ellis raised the small matter of the 82 families and 300 people who would be displaced and cleared off their land. Mr Chamberlain replied to this, saying, 'The only land the Corporation will take possession of is where it is necessary for the creation of a reservoir; and as regards the other land, the Corporation will be very glad to have tenants'. Mr Ellis then repeated, 'I am only going by the notice of the Corporation, in which they say that 82 families will be dispossessed – will be actually displaced from their land; and, in addition to that, I notice that they propose to take a church, two chapels, a school, and one or two burial grounds'. He went on to state that half of the area the Corporation wished to take was common land and that, under the 1876 Enclosure Act, common land was regulated most carefully, suggesting that Birmingham's actions were nothing more than a giant Enclosure Bill:

> I find that 10,000 acres of common will be enclosed in one county, and that in another 20,000 acres will be enclosed. In one common there are 116 occupiers, and in the other 172, so that these powers concern 300 farmers with comparatively small farms. They have the right of common pasture upon these mountains, and with it they can live with comparative thrift and in comfort; but without it life would be impossible.

He went on to mention public access, saying, 'regulations should be made either by the County Council or the Corporation with regard to keeping all the source of that supply pure and uncontaminated; but, over and above these regulations, it seems they should continue the same right of access to these districts as hitherto'. He also wanted fishing protected, but pointed out that, 'the right Hon. Gentleman says that there is no common right of fishing in these rivers and tributaries; but one thing is certain, and that is that there is an immemorial custom on the subject'.

Mr Joseph Bailey, MP for Hereford, then raised the point that the Bill was opposed by five counties: those of Radnorshire, Breconshire, Montgomeryshire, Herefordshire and Worcestershire. He complained that the Bill had been promoted for Birmingham alone without consulting the interests of others, stating his belief that Mr Chamberlain should have come to the House to confirm that, 'We have consulted every interest which will be affected, and have come to ask for this water with the goodwill and approval of all'.

During the debate, the interests of small farmers in particular were raised by Mr Shaw Lefevre, MP for Bradford. Mr Chamberlain had already made references that the Bill should go before a Select Committee, when Mr Lefevre stood up to make the point that he wished the small farmers to have ample opportunity to be heard before the Committee. These farmers were not commoners. They were tenants of landlords who themselves were commoners, so the tenant farmers had no common rights. What Mr Lefevre wished was that they be heard and their rights respected. He went on to say,

> I desire that the Committee should have power to summon these people before them and to pay their expenses. I understand from my right Hon. Friend, the Member for West Birmingham, that he is prepared to concede my Instruction if the Welsh Members will not vote against the Bill.

Some Members suggested that the Bill be referred to a larger Committee which would have more powers than an ordinary Select Committee. There being no objections, it was moved that the Bill be referred to a Hybrid Committee.

On 11 **March 1892**, the House sat again, and it was ordered that the Bill go before a Committee of nine Members; that all petitions against the Bill be presented three clear days before the Committee sat, and that the Committee have the power to call for persons, papers and records.

At the 11 March sitting, Mr Shaw Lefevre again raised his point about the rights of the small farmers and tenants. He said, 'the small farmers I have alluded to are, in the main, very poor men. They have no means whatever of appearing before the Committee, by counsel or otherwise; they have not even petitioned Parliament against the Bill, though I am told on good authority that they are unanimously opposed to this scheme.' He also raised the subject of enclosure of the land, and stated, 'The compensation for enclosure does not, as a rule, go to the small farmers for the extinction of their rights; it goes to the landowner of whom the small farmer is tenant, and the latter gets no compensation.'

Mr Chamberlain remarked, 'My right Hon. Friend has made a very long speech over a very small point', and suggested that the men he referred to – who were, at present, struggling to make a poor living out of the land – 'will find much to their advantage in having a Corporation spending millions in their immediate neighbourhood, and I am sure that nobody would regret more than these men, for whom the right Hon. Gentleman speaks, if anything should happen to defeat the Bill'.

Mr A.J. Williams, MP for Glamorgan South, raised the question of who was going to pay for the commoners and tenant farmers to raise petitions against the Bill, and suggested that the cost should be met by the promoters of the Bill, but this was received with laughter.[1]

On 30 **March**, the *South Wales Daily News* reported that the Welsh Members were considering what action to take concerning the formation of the Hybrid Committee, as Wales was totally unrepresented on the Committee, and some of the remaining Members were said to have close interests in the Bill. In consequence, the Welsh Members decided to raise the matter in the House. The *Daily News* also reported that Mr Evan Williams of Bryntirion, Rhayader had been seen in the lobby of the House, and was actively interested in preserving those rights of commoners, tenants and inhabitants, who would be affected by the Bill (Mr Samuel Charles Evan Williams was a former High Sheriff and Liberal MP for Radnor and, at the time, an Alderman and County Magistrate. He would be named amongst a group of petitioners against the Bill, all of whom were owners of property along the proposed line of the pipe).

On 31 **March**, the Hybrid Committee sat for the first time, and there were 36 petitions brought against the Bill. These included ones from: Mrs Anne Sladen of Rhydoldog; Edward David Thomas and Rhys Llewellyn Williams, who were joint-owners of Rhiwnant and Nant-y-Car; Sir Joseph Bailey, owner of land upon the watershed; Robert Lewis Lloyd of Nant-Gwyllt; Builth Lead Mining Company; Maria Maude Prickard of Dderw; Edward Wood; Radnorshire County Council; Breconshire County Council and the Radnorshire Highways Board. All of the petitions covered the points raised in the debate in the House of Commons. Along with these went Stephen Williams' proof of evidence in support of the Bill, in which he gave answers to the points raised in the petitions. The Committee sat continuously for eight days and heard evidence from various people.

On 1 **April** the estate of Nant-Gwyllt was discussed, and Mr Pember, who was appearing for Robert Lewis Lloyd, put it to Sir Thomas Martineau (the Mayor of Birmingham and Chairman of the Water Committee) that Mr Lewis Lloyd's estate would be virtually obliterated under the scheme, along with the hamlet nearby. In reply, Sir Thomas said, 'Yes, but I have heard that 180 persons are all who live about Caban Coch'.

Mr Pember replied, 'As I say, that may not sound much to Birmingham, but it may be a good deal to a gentleman living in a private part of Wales, and you swamp the church and the schools'. Sir Thomas responded that he knew the area and there were many sites on Mr Lewis Lloyd's remaining lands where he could build a new mansion.

Another interesting point was raised by Mr John Lloyd, who was appearing on behalf of other petitioners living on the watershed. This time, Mr Edward Lawley Parker (a Member of the Water Committee) was asked about Clause 14 of the Bill (*see pp. 30–32*), in which it stated that if artisans or labourers are turned out from their homes, houses must be found to replace the ones taken. Mr Parker agreed, 'That is so'. Mr Lloyd then raised the question, 'Supposing you turned out tenant farmers from their farms in this area, would you be prepared to do the same and find them alternative homesteads in the neighbourhood?' Mr Parker replied, 'No, I do not suppose we should'. Some members of the Committee seemed to be under the impression that the tenant farmer would come under the same clause, but Mr Lloyd said that they would not. This was put to Mr Parker by Mr Lloyd: 'Would you agree to a clause, if you thought it fair, that tenant farmers should be found places if turned out?'

Mr Parker replied, 'Do you mean to say find farms for the tenants elsewhere?'

'Yes', replied Mr Lloyd.

Mr Parker followed with, 'No, I do not think we should be prepared to enter into that'.

On 4 **April**, midway through the Hybrid Committee hearings, the subject of Nant-Gwyllt came up again, this time while James Mansergh (Civil Engineer) was being questioned. Mr Mansergh remarked that he had tried to devise a scheme which would not submerge Mr Lewis Lloyd's home, but he found that it could not be done, and that the scheme would not work without putting a dam at Caban-coch, meaning that Nant-Gwyllt would be covered by 40 or 50 feet of water. He went on to say that if a water supply was to come from these valleys – whoever undertook it, be it Birmingham, London or South Wales – then Nant-Gwyllt would be drowned.

When asked if any of the land to be taken was cultivated, Mr Mansergh said, 'Only in the bottom of the valleys around Caban-coch and Nant-Gwyllt, and a little way up each arm of the Caban reservoir, amounting to about 1,500 acres out of a total of 45,000 acres to be taken; otherwise it is open sheep walk'.

The question of local industry was also addressed during the hearing, and the Committee was told that the only operational industry in the area, aside from shepherding, was a small mine at Nant-y-Carw. This, according to Mr Mansergh, 'will die, like all other lead mines in the district have died'.

On 7 April, towards the end of the hearings, Stephen Williams (County Surveyor and Land Agent) appeared before the Committee. He was asked a number of questions, and gave a breakdown of the population of the watershed area, amounting to 362 men, women and children:

> Of heads of families 34 are farmers, or farmers and shepherds. By that I mean shepherds that occupy land more or less in conjunction with their shepherding for other people. The others are farmers. 27 are miners employed by the Builth Mining Company, and consequently are a floating population, and there are 12 labourers or shepherds, who are simply ordinary weekly labourers or daily labourers. The remainder of the population is made up of the family of the squire of the parish, Mr. Robert Lewis Lloyd, of his keepers and servants, and one or two small tradespeople.

The subject of tenants came up again when Mr Williams was being questioned by Edward Wood, a Rhayader solicitor. Mr Wood asked if tenants were covered by the Land Clauses Consolidation Act (which covers the compulsory purchase of land). Mr Williams stated that, if you deprive an occupier of his holding, he is entitled to the unexpired interest in the holding under the Act. Mr Wood then said, 'As a fact, do not you know that every single tenant on the watershed area is only a yearly tenant – a tenant from year to year?'

Mr Williams replied, 'then what complaint has he?'

Mr Wood went on to state that, if Birmingham acquired the land and gave tenants notice of 12 months to quit, they would receive no compensation whatsoever. Mr Williams said they would be covered by the Agricultural Holdings Act, but Mr Wood informed him that the Act did not apply in most of these cases.

Mr Wood went on to ask about the number of dwellings on the watershed. Mr Williams had been provided with a list from the civil engineer James Mansergh, which stated that there were 62 dwellings, of which 33 would be affected. He then asked if it had been suggested that any of those 33 properties be replaced: Mr Williams had no suggestion to make on the matter. Mr Wood then pointed out that these dwellings could not be replaced as there was a prohibition contained in the Birmingham Corporation Water Bill on erecting buildings on the watershed.[2]

An interesting point to note here is that during this evidence, which took place on 7 April, it was mentioned that both Sir Joseph Bailey and Robert Lewis Lloyd had withdrawn their opposition to the Bill.

On **8 April**, the *South Wales Echo* reported that the Hybrid Committee had sat again and taken further evidence. The opposition of certain commoners had been withdrawn on agreement with the Birmingham Corporation and the Committee had adjourned.

Back in the House of Commons on 4 April the matter of there being no Welsh interest on the Committee had been discussed. It was suggested that the Committee should be increased in number and that the likely additions would be Mr T. Ellis (Merionethshire) and Mr Kenyon (Denbighshire). Mr Chamberlain, the MP for Birmingham West, said that he had no objection, but felt the matter should have all been dealt with when the Members of the original Committee were chosen. He also complained of the timing of the motion to add to the Committee when it had already commenced its sittings and had started its examinations. In a strange statement he also said, 'Welsh Members have really a small interest in the Bill, and I am sure their constituents will be very dissatisfied if the Bill is lost in consequence of the action of their Representatives'. Mr Osbourne Morgan, MP for Denbighshire East, replied, 'I should have thought that if there was one part of the United Kingdom which ought to be represented on such a Committee it would be the locality from which the water is proposed to be taken'.[3]

On **2 May**, after the Easter recess, the Committee reconvened and further evidence was heard from Welsh opposers of the Bill – including local sheep farmer Edward Thomas and Rhayader churchwarden John Powell Williams. The clauses of the Bill were looked at again, and amendments were made giving 21-year leases to tenants who occupied land, if they wished, retaining their rights to cut turf, but under regulation to protect water supply and to provide suitable places for sheep washing.

On **6 May** the *South Wales Daily News* reported that Mr Wood had announced that the Welsh tenants and occupiers had come to an arrangement with the Corporation, which had now agreed not to disturb them and to give them 21-year leases at the same rent, and allow them to remain in possession of all land not required for the reservoirs.

Mr Wood went on to say that he now had to withdraw the petition as the tenants and occupiers were perfectly satisfied. By 18 May the clauses had been dealt with and the Bill was then reported to the House of Commons.

On **23 May**, a meeting took place in Rhayader, attended by inhabitants of the district. At this, a resolution was passed that, while they were satisfied that the greater part of the wastelands would remain open, they wished to protest at the threatened loss of their immemorial privileges previously enjoyed, and to call on Parliament to safeguard those privileges. The inhabitants also stated their wish that any bye-laws required should be made by the local authority. Mr Evan Williams (Bryntirion) was present and again made the point that the tenant farmers whose property was to be submerged had not been fairly treated by the Corporation.[4] It can be seen from this meeting that the residents were still very unhappy. Yet despite this, according to the Hybrid Committee, all was well.

On **24 May**, the *South Wales Daily News* reported that the Birmingham Water Bill was up for further consideration in a few days' time, and that Mr Ellis had put down amendments to secure compensation and goodwill for tenants, further amendments to secure fishing rights in the upper reservoirs that are to be constructed as compensation for the loss of their rights to fish in the streams which are to be lost to those reservoirs, and for the making of bye-laws.

On **26 May**, the House sat to consider these and other amendments. On the subject of 21-year leases it seems that some Members thought that the Birmingham Corporation was being very generous in these matters; however, Mr Ellis was of the opinion that, while he had no doubt that liberal compensation would be given to the landowners, the granting of 21-year leases to tenants was the very least that should be done. He went on to add an appeal to Mr Chamberlain saying, 'that liberal compensation shall be given to tenants who are to be turned from their homes after occupation extending over thirty, forty, and even in some cases more than seventy, years'.

Mr Chamberlain stated that he would give consideration to any suggestions that Mr Ellis had made, but was sure the tenants had been fully heard at the Committee, and were satisfied with what the Corporation proposed to do for them. He assured Mr Ellis, however, that if there was any hole in these proposals the Corporation would give it their fullest consideration.

On **31 May**, the Bill was read for a third time. Further discussion followed and attempts were made to delay the Bill, before the Bill was finally passed.[5]

The following confidential letter was sent to Mr Stephen Williams, County Surveyor and Land Agent, from Mr Edward Lawley Parker, a Member of the Water Committee, on the 3 June 1892. The friend mentioned is not identified, but it can be seen, even at this late stage, that local feelings continued to run high, with some people remaining far from satisfied.[6]

Copy

City of Birmingham
Mayors Parlour
The Council House

June 3rd 1892

Dear Mr Stephen Williams

Our Rhayader friend (or enemy) is on the war path again and fresh grievances are being created to order !

It has struck me that it might be well to consider the cases of the tenants disturbed through the reservoirs coming into their farms and (seeing that they would get a 21 years lease if they remained) give them some compensation for disturbance if they lose any of their land. Before bringing this matter to the Committee I shall be glad if you will let me know :-

1st   How many such cases are there on the whole area ?

2nd   Extent of land required for reservoirs in each case ?

3rd   On which reservoirs are they ?

4th   Define cases, if any where the whole of the holding is taken ?

If you can send me this information by Tuesday I shall be much obliged to you. We hope to get into Committee about Wednesday June 15th and to push the Bill through before the dissolution but are not over sanguine.

The Rhayader ultimatum is said to be as follows:-

1st   Free fishing in upper Reservoirs and above and in natural lakes.

2nd   Tenants disturbed for Reservoirs, first required, to be compensated as though they held leases.

3rd   Scenery Clause – Pipes to be below surface after crossing the Wye.

It is said that local feeling is very strong and those anxious to preserve peace and safety of the works advise a settlement !

If you can give me any information gathered from your own observation I shall be glad. Please treat this in confidence. The opposition is only serious as causing delay at a critical time.

Yours truly

(*signed*) Lawley Parker

Three further readings took place in the House of Lords, amendments and minor alterations made, and on 21 June 1892 those amendments brought before the House of Commons were agreed to. The following day the Bill was given Royal Assent and became known as the Birmingham Corporation Water Act 1892.

BIRMINGHAM CORPORATION WATER ACT 1892

With the passing of the Act, the final wording of a number of its clauses says much about the arguments raised during the parliamentary debates, and reveals much about how the Act would affect the lives of the people of the Elan and Claerwen valleys.

CLAUSE 14

Restrictions on Displacing Persons of Labouring Class

(*1*) The Corporation shall not under the powers by this Act granted purchase or acquire in any parish ten or more houses which after the passing of this Act have been or on the fifteenth day of December last were occupied either wholly or partially by persons belonging to the labouring class as tenants or lodgers unless or until –

> (*a*) They shall have obtained the approval of the Local Government Board to a scheme for providing new dwellings for such number of persons as were residing in such houses on the fifteenth day of December last or for such number of persons as the Local Government Board shall after enquiry deem necessary having regard to the number of persons on or after that date residing in such houses and working within one mile therefrom and to the amount of vacant suitable accommodation in the immediate neighbourhood of such houses or to the place of employment of such persons and to all the circumstances of the case; and

> (*b*) They shall have given security to the satisfaction of the Local Government Board for the carrying out of the scheme.

(*2*) The approval of the Local Government Board to any scheme under this section may be given either absolutely or conditionally and after the Local Government Board have approved of any such scheme they may from time to time approve either absolutely or conditionally of any modifications in the scheme.

(*3*) Every scheme under this section shall contain provisions prescribing the time within which it shall be carried out and shall require the new dwellings proposed to be provided under the scheme to be completed fit for occupation before the persons residing in the houses in respect of which the scheme is made are displaced:

> Provided that the Local Government Board may dispense with the last-mentioned requirement subject to such conditions (if any) as they may see fit.

(*4*) Any provisions of any scheme under this section or any conditions subject to which the Local Government Board may have approved of any scheme or of any modifications of any scheme or subject to which they may have dispensed with the above-mentioned requirement shall be enforceable by a writ of Mandamus [*an order from a superior court*] to be obtained by the Local Government Board out of the High Court.

(*5*) If the Corporation acquire or appropriate any house or houses under the powers by this Act granted in contravention of the fore-going provisions or displace or cause to be displaced the persons residing in any house or houses in contravention of the requirements of the scheme they shall be liable to a penalty of five hundred pounds in respect of every such house which penalty shall be recoverable by the Local Government Board by action in the High Court and shall be carried to and form part of the Consolidated Fund of the United Kingdom provided that the court may if it think fit reduce such penalty.

(*6*) For the purpose of carrying out any scheme under this section the Corporation may appropriate any lands for the time being belonging to them or which they have power to acquire:

Provided that nothing in this section shall relieve the Corporation from the necessity of obtaining the approval of the Local Government Board for such appropriation or use of their corporate land as would acquire such approval under the Municipal Corporations Act 1882 (as amended by section 72 of the Local Government Act 1888) or any other general Act.

(*7*) Subject to the provisions of this section the Corporation and the Local Government Board and their inspectors shall have and may exercise for any purpose in connection with any scheme under this section all or any of the powers vested in them under the Public Health Acts in the same manner in every respect as if the preparation and carrying into effect of such scheme were one of the general purposes of the said Acts:

Provided that all lands on which any buildings have been erected or provided by the Corporation in pursuance of any scheme under this section shall for a period of twenty-five years from the passing of this Act be appropriated for the purpose of dwellings and every conveyance demise or lease of such lands and buildings shall be endorsed with notice of this enactment:

Provided also that the Local Government Board may at any time dispense with all or any of the requirements of this sub-section subject to such conditions (if any) as they may see fit.

(*8*) The Corporation shall pay to the Local Government Board a sum to be fixed by that Board in respect of the preparation and issue of any Provisional Order in pursuance of this section and any expenses incurred by that Board in relation to any enquiries under this section including the expenses of any witnesses summoned by the inspector holding the enquiry and a sum to be fixed by that Board not exceeding three guineas a day for the services of such inspector.

(*9*) For the purposes of this section the expression "labouring class" includes mechanics artizans labourers and others working for wages hawkers costermongers persons not working for wages but working at some trade or handicraft without employing others except members of their own family and persons other than domestic servants whose income does not exceed an average of thirty shillings a week and the families of any such persons who may be residing with them.

[*The definitions of the old-fashioned terms used in the above section are as follows: 'mechanic': manual labourer; 'artizan': skilled craftsman; 'hawker' and 'costermonger': sellers of items such as handicrafts or foodstuffs, who may, in the case of the hawker, travel around with their goods*].

CLAUSE 15
Provisions for Corporation granting long leases in certain cases

(*1*) In cases where the Corporation shall have acquired under the powers of this Act a freehold interest in the soil of any which are not intended for the site of any work and are not within the limits of deviation for any work authorised by this Act they shall if thereunto required in manner hereinafter required provided by the person from whom such freehold interest was acquired grant to him a lease of such lands exclusive of any mines or minerals under the same for nine hundred and ninety-nine years at a rate equal to three per centum per annum on the capital value of the lands comprised in the lease exclusive as aforesaid.

(*2*) This section does not extend to any lands over which any common or commonable rights exist or which form part of any manor.

(*3*) Any difference as to the value of any mines or minerals or as to any other matter or thing arising under this section shall be settled by arbitration.

(*4*) This section applies only to lands situate in the counties of Cardigan Radnor Brecknock and Montgomery.

CLAUSE 16
Procedure for obtaining lease

The owner of any freehold interest in any such lands who desires to avail himself of the provisions of the last preceding section must within six months after the passing of this Act if before its passing he has entered into a provisional agreement with the Corporation for the purchase of his interest and in any other case within six months after notice to treat under the Land Clauses Acts or the execution of an agreement for purchase serve on the Corporation notice of such his desire and it shall be the duty of the Corporation to grant him such a lease as aforesaid containing such covenants as may be necessary or expedient for the prevention or regulation of any act or thing tending to the pollution of any waters which the Corporation are authorised to collect divert or impound under any of the provisions of this Act or tending to the injury of the waterworks of the Corporation with a proviso of re-entry in case of a breach of any such covenant but the right of re-entry shall be subject to the restrictions and relief provided by section 14 of the Conveyancing and Law of Property Act 1881.

Any difference between the Corporation and the owner as to the necessity or expediency of any such covenant as aforesaid shall be settled by the Board of Agriculture and that Board may direct any expenses incurred by them under this section to be paid wholly by the Corporation or wholly by the owner or by the Corporation and the owner in such proportions as the Board shall see fit to direct and the Board may recover the amount of any expenses directed to be so paid in any court of competent jurisdiction.

CLAUSE 17
Corporation to grant leases to present tenants

(*1*) The Corporation shall grant leases for terms of twenty-one years to all tenants who may desire the same and who at the time of the passing of this Act may be in occupation of any lands which the Corporation may under the provisions of this Act acquire other than lands within the limits of deviation shown upon the deposited plans in respect of the reservoirs and works by this Act authorised and the rent of such lands under such leases shall be the same as that paid by such tenants respectively at the passing of this Act and such tenants shall be entitled under such leases to the same terms and conditions as those under which they at present hold and occupy such lands Provided always that in any case where a portion of the land now occupied by any such tenants is situate within the said limits of deviation he shall be entitled to a proportionate reduction in respect of the land within the said limits in the amount of the rent to be paid under such lease and as to any land within the said limits the tenants shall be allowed to hold and occupy such lands as at present and on the same terms as to rent and otherwise until such period as the Corporation may require the same for the purpose of their works.

(*2*) The said leases shall contain such covenants as may be necessary or expedient for the prevention or regulation of any act or thing tending to the pollution of any waters which the Corporation are authorised to collect divert or impound under any of the provisions of this Act or tending to the injury of the waterworks of the Corporation with a proviso of re-entry in case of non-payment of rent or a breach of any of the covenants but the right of re-entry shall be subject to the restrictions and relief provided by section 14 of the Conveyancing and Law of Property Act 1881.

(*3*) The Corporation shall recompense any tenant for any loss sustained or expense incurred by alteration or change in respect of sheep washing places and in case of difference the same shall be determined by two justices of the peace.

(*4*) Provided that this section shall not apply to any lands in respect of which the owner exercises the option taking a lease under the section of this Act with the marginal note "Provisions for Corporation granting long leases in certain cases" nor shall any tenant be entitled to demand a lease under this section until after the expiration of the time limited for the exercise of the option under the said section.

(5) This section applies only to lands within the counties of Cardigan Radnor Brecknock and Montgomery.

Clause 24
Removal of bodies from Carig Ddu Baptist Chapel graveyard

The Corporation shall cause the remains of any person interred or deposited in any portion of the graveyard attached to Carig Ddu Baptist Chapel in the parish of Llansantffraid-cwm-deuddwr in the county of Radnor which they may acquire under the powers of this Act to be removed under the superintendence of the medical officer of health for the said county and interred in some other unconsecrated ground where burials may legally take place and shall cause any monuments and tombstones in any such portion of the grave-yard to be removed to and fixed or re-erected Provided that the heirs executors adminis-trators or relations or friends of any person whose remains shall be interred or deposited in such graveyard may if they so prefer (at the cost of the Corporation such cost not to exceed ten pounds in each case) and under such superintendence as aforesaid remove the remains of such person to any burial ground wherein burials may legally take place and remove the monument or tombstone erected to the memory of such person to any place they may think fit.

Clause 48
Prohibition of sheep washing

If in the opinion of the Corporation it shall be expedient with the view of preserving the purity of the water to prohibit the washing of sheep in any of the waters which the Corporation are authorised to impound or take under the provisions of this Act the Corporation shall have power to prohibit such washing of sheep provided that before the Corporation carry this provision into effect in respect of any place where it has been practice to wash sheep the Corporation shall provide and maintain in the nearest convenient situation on their own lands another suitable washing place and enclosure and shall also provide means of pasturage for such sheep during such period as may be necessary to keep such sheep at the washing places and on their coming and return and shall provide the necessary accommodation for the shepherds accompanying the flocks.

Clause 49
Drinking places for cattle

The Corporation shall provide suitable and convenient drinking places for cattle sheep and horses in case it shall become necessary for them to interfere with existing drinking places on any lands acquired by them under this Act.

CLAUSE 50

Power to make byelaws

(*1*) The Corporation may as respects any common or unenclosed land acquired by them in the parishes of Yspytty-Ystwyth in the county of Cardigan Llanwrthwl in the county of Brecknock and Llansantffraid-cwmdeuddwr in the county of Radnor and the parish of Llangurig in the county of Montgomery make byelaws for the protection of their waterworks and for prevention of pollution of the water to be collected diverted or impounded from such lands and for preservation of order among persons resorting thereto.

(*2*) The byelaws may without prejudice to the generality of the foregoing words include all or any of the following purposes (that is to say):–

The regulation of the time place and mode of digging and taking turf from the said lands and the cutting of heather bracken or gorse thereon;

The regulation of fishing and recreation on the said lands and of assemblages of persons thereon;

Generally the prevention of nuisances and the prevention or regulation of any act or thing tending to pollution of the water to be collected diverted or impounded by the Corporation or to the injury of their waterworks.

(*3*) Sections 16 and 17 of the Commons Act 1876 shall apply to all byelaws made by the Corporation under this section with the substitution of the Board of Agriculture for one of Her Majesty's Principal Secretaries of State and the Corporation for conservators Provided that a copy of the proposed byelaws shall be sent to the clerk of the council of each county within which the byelaws are intended to operate one month at least before application is made for their confirmation And if any such county council shall within the said month apply to the Board of Agriculture for a local inquiry it shall not be lawful for that Board to confirm the proposed byelaws until after the holding of such inquiry and the provisions of section 11 of the Commons Act 1876 shall so far as the same in the judgement of the Board are applicable apply to such local inquiry and the expenses incurred by the Board in relation thereto shall be borne by the county council and the Corporation in such proportions or wholly by the one or wholly by the other as the Board may certify.

CLAUSE 51

Compensation to commoners injuriously affected by the restrictions or byelaws

The Corporation shall pay compensation to any owner commoner or other person injuriously affected by the restrictions or byelaws imposed by or made under the provisions of this Act and such compensation shall be settled by two justices in accordance with the provisions of the Land Clauses Acts as in the case of claims for compensation under section 22 of the Lands Clauses Consolidation Act 1845.

CLAUSE 52

As to purchase of settle flocks on lands acquired by Corporation in the counties Cardigan Radnor or Brecknock

In any case where sheep are settled and depastured on any lands acquired by the Corporation under the provisions of this Act in any parish in the counties of Cardigan Radnor Brecknock or Montgomery or in respect of which the owner of such sheep exercises commonable rights in the same parish the Corporation shall if the owners of such sheep so require shall purchase the same at a price to be settled on the basis of the value of a settled flock according to the custom of the country and as between incoming and outgoing tenant and as if such purchase were a compulsory purchase and in the case of difference such price and all other matters in difference shall be settled by arbitration by a fit person to be appointed by the county council of the county in which such sheep are settled and depastured on the application of the Corporation or of the owner of such sheep. The expression "settled and depastured" in the section shall apply only to sheep settled and depastured for not less than one year on any commonable land acquired by the Corporation or on any land to which such commonable land is appurtenant.

CLAUSE 53

Access to commons

The public shall be entitled to a privilege at all times of enjoying air exercise and recreation on such parts of any common or unenclosed land acquired by the Corporation in the parishes of Yspytty-Ystwyth in the county of Cardigan Llanwrthwl in the county of Brecknock and Llansantffraid-cwmdeuddwr in the county of Radnor and the parish of Llangurig in the county of Montgomery (and whether any common or commonable rights in or over such lands shall have been acquired or extinguished under the provisions of this Act or not) as shall not be included within the limits of deviation for works mentioned in this Act subject nevertheless to the provisions of and to the byelaws authorised by this Act.

CLAUSE 54

As to fishing rights

All rights of fishing in the rivers Elan and Claerwen and their tributaries flowing through the manor of Grange and the manor of Builth above the upper end of the upper reservoirs and in the lakes adjacent thereto hitherto enjoyed by the inhabitants of the district and the town of Rhayader and all rights of turbary [*the right to cut turf or peat*] and of cutting fern and rushes over such commonable land shall be preserved to the said inhabitants as heretofore and without interruption by the Corporation subject nevertheless to the byelaws authorised by this Act.

For the protection of Dderw estate

The following provision shall apply and have effect for the protection of the Dderw estate in the counties of Radnor Brecon and Montgomery of which estate Maria Maude Prickard is or claims to be tenant for life or other the owner or owners for the time being of the said estate or any part thereof who are in this section meant by and included in the expression "the owner":—

(*1*) The owner shall have the sole and exclusive right of fowling shooting and sporting on all lands now belonging to her and which the Corporation may acquire under the powers of this Act and shall also be entitled to the right of fishing with rod and line for any two persons at the same time in the Caban Coch reservoir and also to the right of using a boat on the said reservoir provided that the said boat shall not be let or used for hire but used solely by the owner and her heirs and assigns being such owners as aforesaid and her and their friends and servants. This provision shall terminate at the expiration of twenty-one years from the death of the said Maria Maude Prickard;

(*2*) The Corporation shall not exercise the compulsory power of purchase over the estate of the owner after the expiration of three years from the passing of this Act;

(*3*) The Corporation shall lay down and maintain aqueducts conduits or line of pipes described and authorised by this Act so far as the same may pass through the estate of the owner as nearly as practicable in the line shown as the centre line on the deposited plans and shall not deviate therefrom without the consent in writing of the owner;

(*4*) Notwithstanding anything in this Act contained the Corporation shall not for the purpose of this aqueduct or line of pipes purchase any part of the estate of the owner but they may purchase take and use and the owner may and shall sell and grant to them accordingly an easement or right of using the same for such purposes;

(*5*) The Corporation in constructing the said aqueducts conduits or lines of pipes shall from time to time make provision by culverts or otherwise to the reasonable satisfaction of the owner or her agent for carrying the present and future drainage of the said estate across the same;

(*6*) The Corporation shall reconstruct all fences on the said estate which may be interfered with during the construction of any work and shall from time to time in addition to any other compensation payable by them under this Act in respect of the said estate make full compensation to the owner and her tenants for all damages and loss occasioned by the Corporation their officers or contractors in or about any works of construction or repair or consequent thereon;

(*7*) The Corporation shall not take or divert into the aqueduct any springs streams or running waters on the said estate but shall cause the same to flow as nearly as may be in the same course and at the same level as they do now;

(*8*) The Corporation shall to the reasonable satisfaction of the owner or her agent rein-state all water courses springs or running waters which may be crossed or interfered with under the powers of this Act;

(*9*) It shall be lawful for the owner to form lay out and make along and across the said aqueducts or lines of pipes any occupation roads or paths required by her;

(*10*) All such portions of the aqueduct through the property of the owner as may be made in the form of cut and cover and not of tunnel shall when the work is completed be covered anew with soil or the surplus material and shall be made as nearly as may be to correspond with the adjacent surface of the ground and not to interfere unreasonably or unduly with the natural slope thereof and in no case shall the top of such aqueduct be raised higher on the centre line of such aqueduct than the height thereof shown on the deposited plans and sections and no surplus material from the construction of the aqueduct shall be deposited within the distance of four hundred yards from any resi-dence of the owner without the consent in writing of the owner;

(*11*) No walls or fences shall be erected upon the lands over the aqueduct without the consent in writing of the owner;

(*12*) Except as otherwise agreed between the Corporation and owner the rights of way enjoyed by such owner and her tenants over any land taken or acquired under the powers of this Act shall not be interrupted or interfered with;

(*13*) Any difference which may from time to time arise between the owner and the Corporation with respect to any payment to be made by the Corporation to the owner shall be settled as if such difference were a question of disputed compensation and any money payable under this section by the Corporation to the owner may be recovered in any court of competent jurisdiction.[7]

NOTES

1. *Hansard* 1892 Vol 2, cc 265–307 and cc 608–627. Contains Parliamentary information licensed under the Open Parliament Licence v3.0
2. From Powys County Archives R/D/WWA/1/146–164 Petitions against Bill, and R/D/LEW/2/655–663 Minutes of Evidence Hybrid Committee
3. *Hansard* 1892 Vol 3 cc 536–552. Contains Parliamentary information licensed under the Open Parliament Licence v3.0
4. Powys County Archives R/D/WWA/1/39
5. *Hansard* 1892 Vol 4 cc 1857–83 and Vol 5 cc 337–48. Contains Parliamentary information licensed under the Open Parliament Licence v3.0
6. Transcribed from Powys County Archives R/D/WWA/1/39
7. From Powys County Archives R/D/LEW/2/663

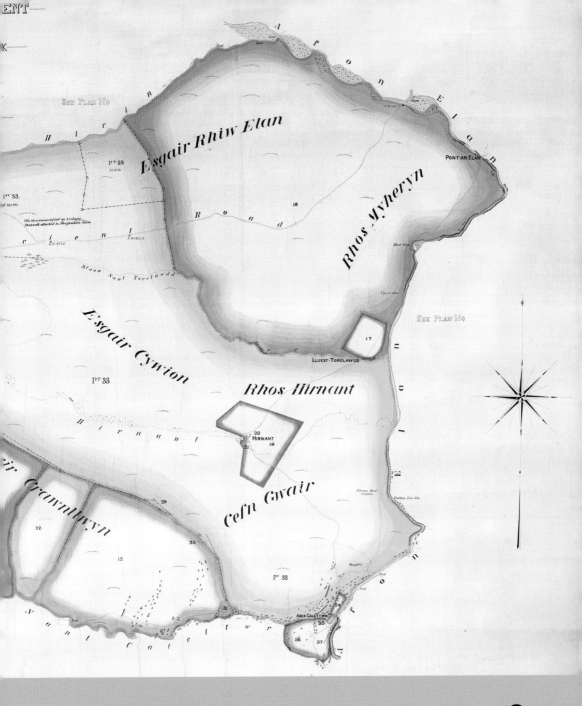

PART **3**

Building the Dams

☞

Detail of Terrier Plan "H", by surveyor John Jones, 1902(?), showing a number of the properties in the northern part of the watershed, including Lluest–Torclawdd and Aber–Calettwr, which would be lost to the Craig-goch reservoir

3

THE SCHEME THAT James Mansergh proposed to the Birmingham Corporation consisted of three reservoirs on the River Elan and a further three reservoirs on the River Claerwen. This would be achieved by the building of the Caban-coch, Pen-y-gareg and Craig-goch dams on the Elan, together with the submerged Gareg-ddu dam. The purpose of the submerged dam is to keep the water level in the upper part of the Caban-coch reservoir at a point that enables the water to enter the inlet to the aqueduct. In times of low water it can be topped up with water from the Pen-y-gareg and Craig-goch reservoirs and also with water from the Claerwen valley via a tunnel from the Dol-y-mynach reservoir. The lower portion of the Caban-coch reservoir, downstream of the submerged dam, is for compensation water to the river.

These works, along with the building of the foundations of the Dol-y-mynach dam on the River Claerwen, the construction of a railway to deliver materials and supplies to the various building sites, and the construction of a 73-mile-long aqueduct to deliver the water to Birmingham, would form the first phase of the scheme. A second phase (to be built at a later date when demand required it) was to entail the completion of the Dol-y-mynach dam and construction of the Cil-oerwynt and Pant-y-beddau dams on the River Claerwen, in order to form the three Claerwen Valley reservoirs envisaged in the scheme (*see plan overleaf, p. 42*).

James Mansergh was appointed by the Corporation to draw up detailed plans in order to carry out his scheme. It was decided that the building of the dams and reservoirs was to be carried out by the Corporation hiring its own labour, but that the building of the railway and aqueduct would be contracted out. Mansergh also recommended the building of a workers' village just below the site of the Caban-coch dam, along with smaller encampments further up the valley for workers employed on the Pen-y-gareg and Craig-goch dams.

PREPARING THE GROUND

The 1892 Water Act gave the Birmingham Corporation the power to acquire the watershed of the two rivers, totalling some 45,562 acres. As far as the relevant landowners were concerned, most had agreed terms with the Corporation, and had sold their property and land by 1895 (one or two took a bit longer due to ongoing disputes, but it seems that all had been settled by 1902).

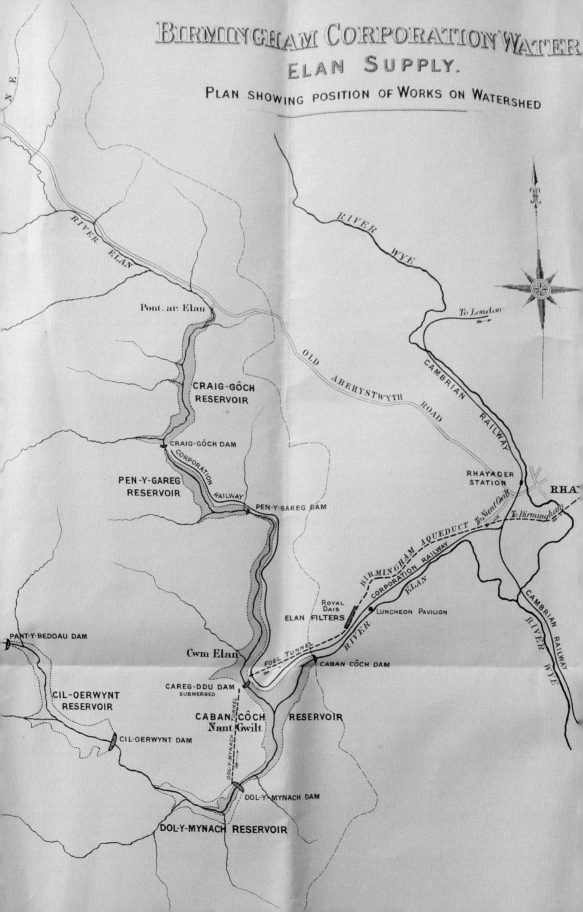

BIRMINGHAM CORPORATION WATER
ELAN SUPPLY.
PLAN SHOWING POSITION OF WORKS ON WATERSHED

RIVER ELAN

RIVER WYE

Pont. ar. Elan

To London

OLD ABERYSTWYTH ROAD

CAMBRIAN RAILWAY

CRAIG-GÔCH RESERVOIR

CRAIG-GÔCH DAM

CORPORATION RAILWAY

RHAYADER STATION

RHA

PEN-Y-GAREG RESERVOIR

PEN-Y-GAREG DAM

BIRMINGHAM AQUEDUCT

To Nant Gwilt

To Birmingham

CORPORATION RAILWAY

ELAN

PANT-Y-BEDDAU DAM

Royal Dais
ELAN FILTERS

Luncheon Pavilion

RIVER ELAN

CAMBRIAN RAILWAY

RIVER WYE

Cwm Elan

Foel Tunnel

CABAN CÔCH DAM

CIL-OERWYNT RESERVOIR

CAREG-DDU DAM
SUBMERGED

CABAN CÔCH RESERVOIR
Nant Gwilt

DOL-Y-MYNACH TUNNEL

CIL-OERWYNT DAM

DOL-Y-MYNACH DAM

DOL-Y-MYNACH RESERVOIR

By far the largest landowner, and the first to sign an agreement, was Robert Lewis Lloyd of Nant-Gwyllt. Negotiations with the Corporation began in March 1892 and were concluded by April. In the agreement it was stated that Mr Lewis Lloyd would receive £150,000 for all his lands; he would also receive 22 shillings per head for all his sheep and he would retain shooting rights over all the land the Corporation would take. Along with this he would be granted the right to free fishing for two rods on all the reservoirs, and to keep a boat on the Caban-coch reservoir – all these rights to remain for his lifetime. Whether Mr Lewis Lloyd's early settlement encouraged other landowners to agree terms it is not known, but they soon followed.

The other landowners received the following amounts: Sir Joseph Bailey, £21,350; Anne Sladen of Rhydoldog, £20,000; The Earl of Lisburne, £16,500; E. David Thomas and Rhys Llewellyn Williams, £16,000; The Prickard family of Dderw, £15,737; Edward Thomas Evans, £5,000; Thomas Pugh Evans, £5,000; Edward and David Thomas, £4,500; Lewis Pugh Pugh, £3,900, and Thomas James Waddingham, £400. In all these cases there would be other sums involved where the Corporation was required to purchase any sheep stocks.

Nant-Gwyllt, the former home of Robert Lewis Lloyd, would be made ready for the use of George Yourdi, the Resident Engineer appointed by the Corporation in 1893 at the recommendation of James Mansergh. The house would also be used to accommodate Water Committee Members and officials when they visited the site and needed to stay over. Cwm-Elan House, also owned by Robert Lewis Lloyd, would be used by engineering staff.

Early in 1893 the Birmingham Corporation appointed Stephen Williams as their Social Estate Agent. Previously employed to make surveys and to prepare evidence during the parliamentary stage which saw the creation of the Act, his role would now be mainly to settle and assign leases.

With the purchase of the watershed, a comprehensive land survey of the parts of the Elan and Claerwen Valleys now owned by the Corporation was undertaken, and a series of plans was produced by Stephen Williams together with another Land Agent and Surveyor, John Jones. These were known as the Terrier Plans ('Terrier' being the term for a catalogue or survey of lands), and these included an index of details of the land that the Corporation had acquired. The Terrier Plans are incredibly detailed and accurate, with the watershed covered by 26 individual plans (and accompanying index book) mostly drawn up in 1893 and 1894 by Stephen Williams. Parts of a number of these plans are reproduced over the following pages, showing in particular the area around the junction of the Rivers Elan and Claerwen, which was the most heavily populated part of the watershed and where the greatest loss of properties to the reservoirs occurred.

OPPOSITE: Plan of the 1892 Works, showing the projected extent of flooding from the proposed reservoirs (*by permission of Powys Archives R/D/WWA/1/59/2–3*)

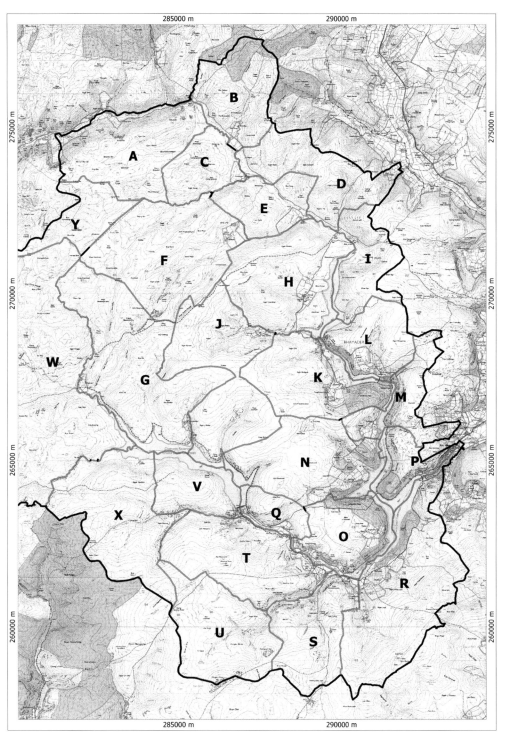

ABOVE: Modern OS map of the watershed. OPPOSITE: *c.1894 index map of the areas covered by the 26 Terrier Plans (by permission of Powys Archives R/DX/62/28 and the Elan Valley Trust)*

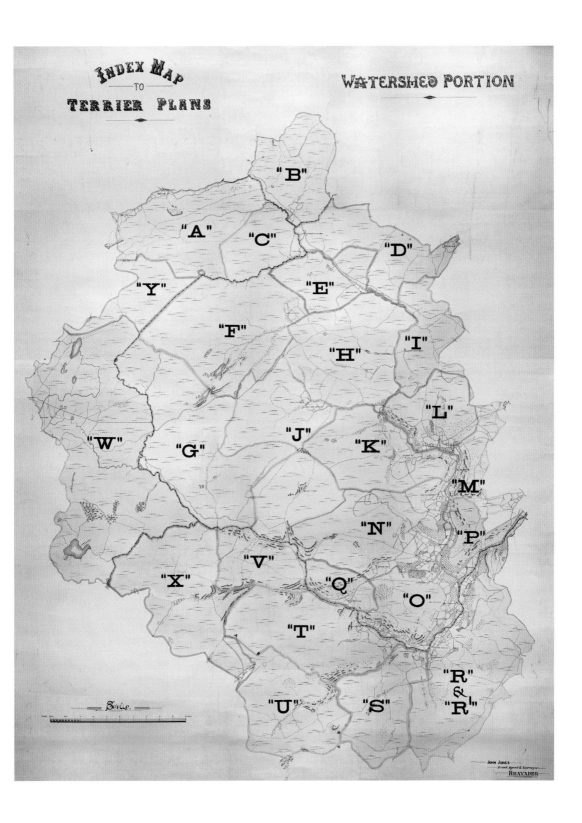

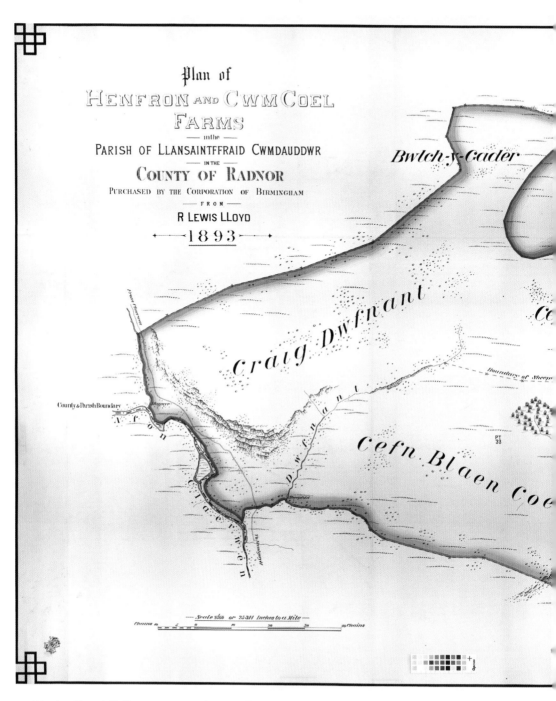

Plan of
HENFRON AND CWM COEL
FARMS
— in the —
PARISH OF LLANSAINTFFRAID CWMDAUDDWR
— IN THE —
COUNTY OF RADNOR
PURCHASED BY THE CORPORATION OF BIRMINGHAM
— FROM —
R LEWIS LLOYD
— 1893 —

Terrier Plan "N" (*by permission of Powys County Archives R/DX/63/28 and the Elan Valley Trust*)

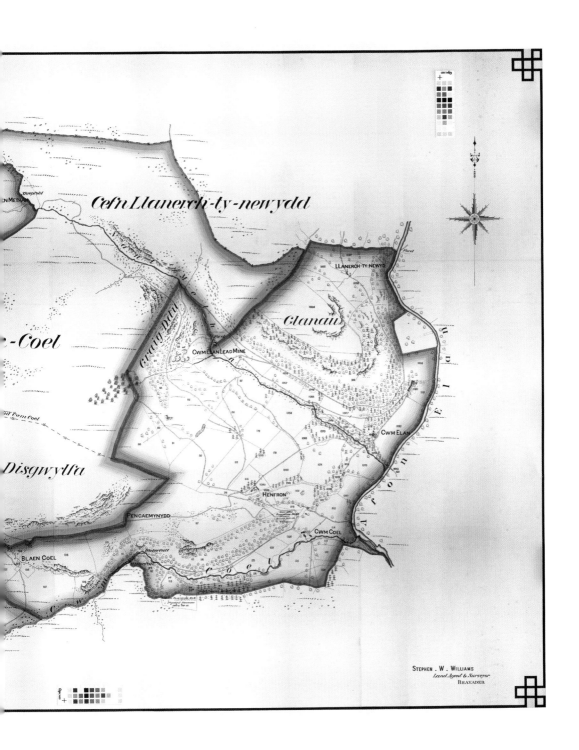

Cefn Llanerch-ty-newydd

Glanau

Craig Ddu

CWM ELAN LEAD MINE

LLANERCH-TY-NEWYD

-Coel

CWM ELAN

Disgwylfa

HENFRON

PENCAEMYNYDD

CWM COEL

BLAEN COEL

STEPHEN . W . WILLIAMS
Land Agent & Surveyor
RHAYADER

ABOVE & OPPOSITE: Details of Terrier Plan "N", showing several properties in the inhabited part of the watershed, and the course of the Elan as it heads south to meet the Claerwen (*by permission of Powys County Archives R/DX/63/28 and the Elan Valley Trust*)

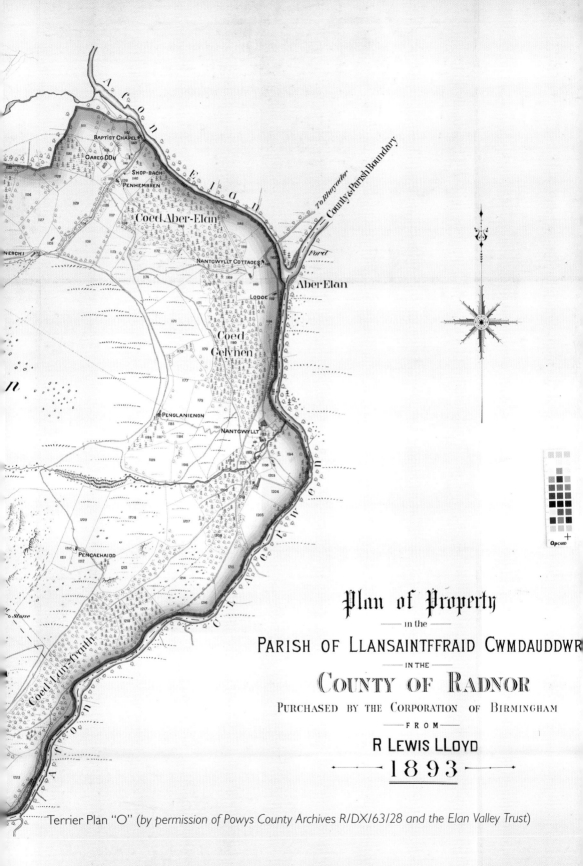

Plan of Property
— in the —
PARISH OF LLANSAINTFFRAID CWMDAUDDWR
— IN THE —
COUNTY OF RADNOR
PURCHASED BY THE CORPORATION OF BIRMINGHAM
— FROM —
R LEWIS LLOYD
— 1893 —

Terrier Plan "O" *(by permission of Powys County Archives R/DX/63/28 and the Elan Valley Trust)*

STEPHEN . W . WILLIAMS
Land Agent & Surveyor
RHAYADER

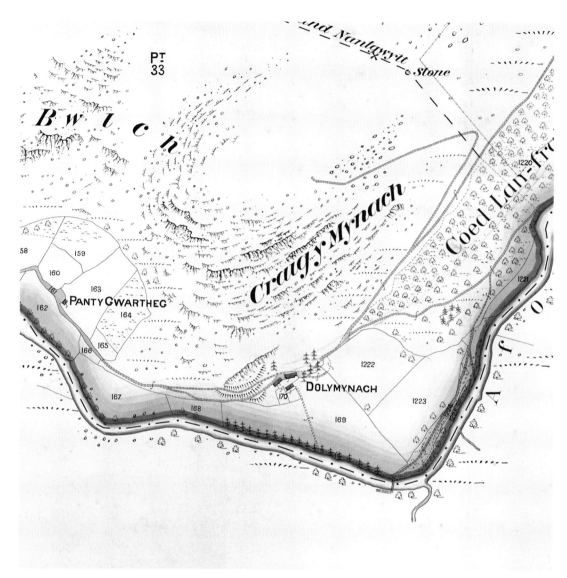

ABOVE & OPPOSITE: Details of Terrier Plan "O", following the course of the Claerwen first eastwards (past Dolymynach) then northwards, up to the Y-shaped junction with the Elan *(by permission of Powys County Archives R/DX/63/28 and the Elan Valley Trust)*

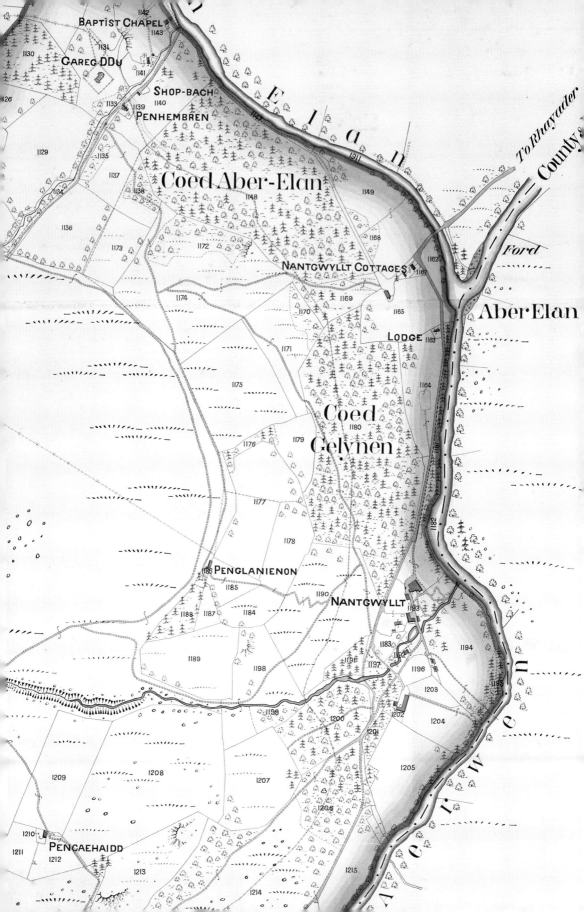

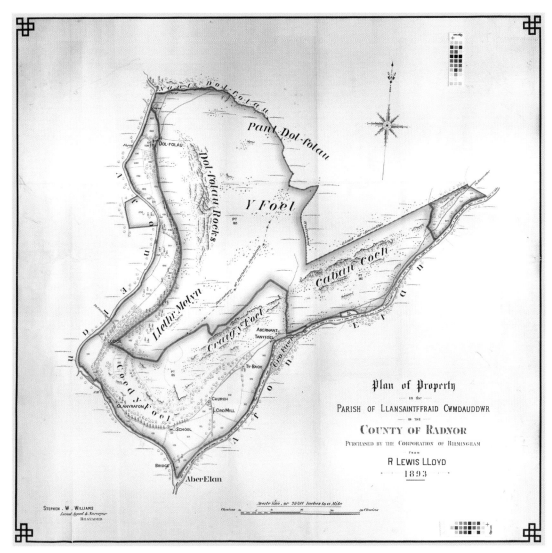

OPPOSITE & ABOVE: Terrier Plan "P" (and detail), showing the further continuation of the River Elan (*by permission of Powys County Archives R/DX/63/28 and the Elan Valley Trust*)

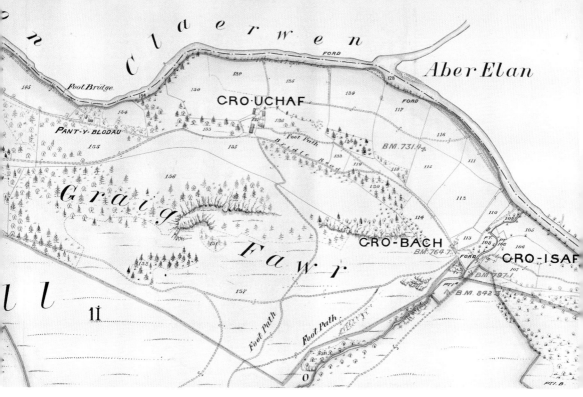

Terrier Plan "R" (and detail), showing properties to the south of the two rivers.
(by permission of Powys County Archives R/DX/63/28 and the Elan Valley Trust)

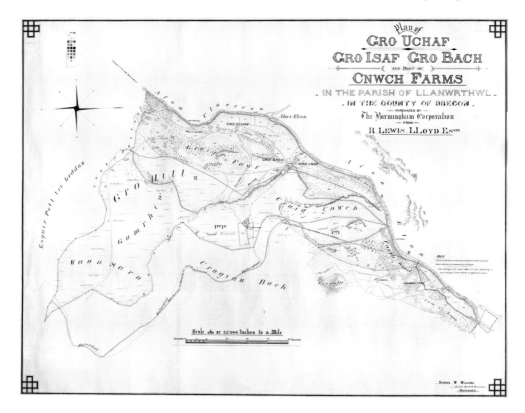

CONSTRUCTION

In 1893 work began on the Elan Valley Railway. This would join up with the pre-existing Cambrian Railway at Rhayader, and by the summer of 1894 the new railway had reached the site of the Caban-coch dam. Work had already begun here on the workers' village and works offices. Dated September 1894, a progress report from James Mansergh to the Corporation stated that construction of the village was well underway: of the 68 Type-1 huts, 32 had been let; 11 of the 23 Type-2 huts were occupied, and 12 of the 28 Type-3 huts were occupied. By this time the railway had reached Caban and work on the next stage of its route had begun. Excavations had begun on the Caban-coch dam, and by then 547 men were at work on the scheme.

By early 1895 the workers' village on the Breconshire side of the River Elan was fully established, with different types of accommodation huts for lodgers (any worker), gangers (foremen) and married men. It also had a School, Mission Room, Hospital, Canteen, Public Baths and a Public Hall. There had been many applications for shops in the village (a number of which were granted) and in 1896 a Fire Station was added. The village had its own water supply from a reservoir created by damming the Nant-y-gro stream, which joined the Elan about half-a-mile upstream of the Caban-coch dam site. A water-powered generator at the base of the Caban dam site provided electricity for the main buildings in the village and for street lighting. The workers' village was reached by a suspension bridge across the river. This was gated and anyone accessing the village needed a pass. Situated opposite the village on the Radnorshire side of the river was a Police Station, a doss-house for new arrivals and an isolation hospital. Workers not housed in the village lodged in local farms, and some of the farms were allowed to erect huts to provide extra accommodation.

Work continued to advance on the railway, and the line reached the Pen-y-gareg site in the spring of 1895, where work soon began on the excavations here. There was some intricate track-work needed to gain access to the site of the Gareg-ddu submerged dam, so work did not begin on the dam here until later that year. The railway continued past Pen-y-gareg, but work here was held up for a while, as a cutting – later known as 'Devil's Gulch' – had to be blasted through the rock. However, by the late spring of 1896 the main railway had reached its terminus at Craig-goch, some eight miles from its start. With the extra track-work needed to access the individual sites, it has been estimated that, in total, there was over 30 miles of new railway track in the area.

In June 1896 work began on the masonry of the submerged Gareg-ddu dam, closely followed in August with the start of work on the Caban-coch dam itself. The excavations at Pen-y-gareg were completed by the end of 1896, and work on the masonry had begun. By the summer of 1897 work had begun on the excavations at Craig-goch, the dam itself being started in April 1898. By the end of 1898 the masonry of the Gareg-ddu dam was complete, and work had begun on the piers to support the viaduct. By now, Phase 1 was well underway, and work would continue simultaneously on all of the dam sites.

Workers on the railway built to bring stone and other materials to the dam construction sites
(*photograph by W.H. Banks, copyright © Hergest Trust Archive*)

Stone for the dams was brought in from two quarries, Gigfran and Cnwch, which were situated on either side of the Caban-coch dam. However, this supply needed to be supplemented with stone from a quarry a few miles south of the site, and stone for the facing of the dams was brought from Pontypridd in South Wales. Cement came all the way from the south-east of England by sea, then by railway to Rhayader and onwards to the site.

Aquaduct

Work on constructing the aqueduct needed to carry the water to Birmingham was started not long after work had begun on the reservoirs, and was contracted out in sections. The aquaduct starts at the Foel tower, just upstream of the Gareg-ddu submerged dam. The Foel tower houses the valves which control the flow of water, and from here the water then travels through the Foel tunnel to the filter beds. The filter beds were not included in James Mansergh's original scheme, but it was decided in 1901 to install them, due to problems that other similar schemes were having with a build-up of peat deposits in the pipeline, which interfered with the water flow. It was proved by a Liverpool water scheme that the use of filtration solved this problem.

From the filter beds, the water enters the aqueduct proper. The aqueduct consists of three types of construction: 'cut and cover' conduit, tunnels and syphon chambers. The 'cut and cover' and tunnel sections are lined with concrete and blue brick, approximately eight feet by seven feet in section, and can handle the full capacity of the scheme. The syphon chambers hold 42-inch diameter pipes, mainly of cast iron. To deal with full capacity, six pipes would be needed, but at the end of the first phase of the scheme only two had been installed (the others being added later when extra capacity was needed).

Work on the first section of the aqueduct, to Dolau, was started in June 1896. The second section would reach Knighton by 1898, and the construction of the remainder would follow in sections across the Midlands, finally ending with the storage reservoir at Frankley in Birmingham. In total, the water would travel 73 miles at a rate of approximately two miles per hour, with an overall drop in elevation of 169 feet.

Equipment

As well as all of the materials and the vast amount of manual labour using pick and shovel, large pieces of heavy machinery were also needed at the dam sites. These included things such as steam cranes, air compressors, steam hammers, crushing plants, stone dressing machines, locomotive engines and trucks, electric engines, pneumatic drills, hydraulic jacks, grinding machines and lathes.

The crushing plants, operated by just seven men, could handle between 80 and 140 tons of stone per day, the stone being delivered in trucks hauled by steam engines. Another labour-saving device, which had many uses, was the compressed air plant, known as a 'wind-jammer': with the use of tubes up to two miles long, power could be delivered to various parts of the site for work such as rock drilling, excavating foundations and operating steam hammers.

Workers

By 1901, the population of the area had increased to 2,143, from 333 in 1891/2. Of these, 1,300 were living in the workers' village. As well as some local people, workers had arrived from the rest of Wales, England, Scotland, Ireland, Guernsey, Jersey, America, Australia, New Zealand, South Africa, Belgium, Italy and Denmark.

Despite all of these people descending on the valley, there seem to have been comparatively few problems. A report in the *Evening Express* of 18 December 1894 describes a fracas after which 150 Welshmen were dismissed and English navvies employed instead. The report went on to say that, 'The question of nationality provokes endless conflict amongst men, and this wholesale dismissal is not calculated to lessen it.' However, another report, this time in the *Montgomeryshire County Times and Shropshire and Mid Wales Advertiser* of 29 December 1894, said there was no truth at all in the alleged dismissal of the men; the newspaper had spoken to the local police, who had said they had very little trouble with the men.

OPPOSITE: Work well advanced on the Pen-y-gareg dam. ABOVE: Work beginning on the Caban-coch dam. OVERLEAF: The Gareg-ddu submerged dam under construction (*photographs by W.H. Banks, copyright © Hergest Trust Archive*)

Pen-y-gareg dam (photograph taken from the opposite bank to the image on p. 60)
(*photograph by W.H. Banks, copyright © Hergest Trust Archive*)

Inevitably, with a construction project of this nature and scale, there would be accidents and fatalities, including the sad case of a young boy, aged 11, who was killed while cleaning a steam crane (the newspapers describing the fatality in graphic detail). Not all deaths were due to the works, however. There were incidents reported in newspapers of an accidental shooting, a suicide and even a murder (the alleged culprit was never identified satisfactorily by witnesses, resulting in the case being dismissed).

The local inhabitants must have been overwhelmed by what they witnessed going on in their valley, seeing the vast numbers of men and machines going about their work, and the massive dams taking shape.

In March 1900, a newspaper article about a visit to the site appeared in the *Towyn-on-Sea & Merioneth County Times*. It was written by David Thomas Hughes, Curate of Machynlleth, who describes the scene:

A VISIT TO THE BIRMINGHAM WATERWORKS

These gigantic works are situated in the Elan Valley, about six or seven miles from Rhayader. The river Elan winds its way between the huge rocks amidst the wildest sceneries of mountains, trees and crags. I had heard a great deal of this Leviathan undertaking and the gigantic scale of the enormous contract; so, having the privilege and pleasure of addressing the Welsh element residing here on St David's Day, I cast my eye around on the following day and surveyed the magnificent views which met the eye on all sides, and the lovely valley below teeming with its thousands of workmen, the valley ere long to become one vast lake to supply the Midland capital with pure crystal water drained from the vast bosoms of the lovely Cymric hills. Although the Birmingham Corporation have a railway running nearly all the way to Rhayader, yet, the weather being perfect and the roads hard and dry, I preferred to walk to Nantgwyllt which is the central portion of the valley, and where most of the workmen live. To describe faithfully the incomparable grandeur of the natural surroundings and to depict accurately the magnitude of the work, would defy the graphic powers of the pen of Bennett Burleigh, but I may be pardoned for presuming to attempt to the many readers of the COUNTY TIMES *a very feint* [sic] *idea of the same, and a glimmer only at the multifarious aspects of this triumph and mastery of human skill over the works of nature. How grandly and loftily the human intellect transcends the works of nature, and suspends natural laws, powerful though they be, in the carrying out of its own unending devices! Evidences of this meet the observant eye on all sides in this wonderful valley of the Elan. This marvellous project, which is to cost nearly eleven million pounds, covers an area of between twelve to fifteen miles. There are three big dams being constructed, and although when completed, they will not perhaps strike the onlooker with such a sense of grandeur and the magnificence of their masonry as the Vyrnwy aqueducts do – which supply the port of Liverpool – yet, upon closer inspection, I venture to say that the Birmingham masonry, as seen in the dams of its huge waterworks at Elan Valley, will be second to none in the United Kingdom, I would say Europe, in the impregnability of its buttresses added to the solidity and size of the work. It is well known to the World that the gentleman of the Corporation of Birmingham are about as level-headed, shrewd, and smart a set of business men as can be met on the face of the earth, and proofs of the ingenuity of their inventive minds stud the valley on all sides. To begin with, this able Corporation of the Midland capital have erected wooden dwellings for about 3,000 working men. I paid a visit to this timber village and was much struck with the cleanliness of its streets, its methodical management by appointed officials, and the comfort and neatness exhibited in the interior of the dwellings. There is only one entrance to this quaint modern village, and before coming to the entrance-gate, which is vigilantly guarded*

by a stalwart keeper – evidently an old Guardsman – a wonderful swing-bridge has to be crossed. In the village all the houses are of wood, tarred outside, of one floor, and a couple of buckets hanging outside each in readiness for fire. There are clerks' huts and engineers' huts, a little apart from those of the workmen. There is a large schoolroom, a hospital, a doss-house, a billiard and reading-room, all of wood, and, to crown all, a huge canteen, open from mid-day until half-past one, and from six in the evening until nine. While this canteen is open four men have their hands full drawing beer as fast they can for these thirsty but hard-working navvies. The Babel of voices while the "pints" are being consumed is something to remember. Extra policemen parade the drinking saloon, but, wonderful to relate, the navvy is very well-behaved as a rule, so long as he gets his "quantum" of beer. The navvy earns five pence-halfpenny an hour, while the stonecutters and mechanics earn 9d an hour, sometimes 10d. They pay the Corporation 5s a week for their houses, but coal is given them free of charge, and, subject to strict conditions, they are allowed to take in lodgers occasionally. The whole valley having been bought by the Corporation from Mr Lloyd of Nantgwyllt Hall for £160,000, every quarry is utilised to its fullest extent. The rocks are drilled for blasting, by steam, and large steam cranes move up and down on rails with mar-vellous rapidity. Large stones, weighing from nine to twelve tons, are moved and shifted about by these powerful cranes, as if they were mere toys. Steam-engines puff away with heavy trucks right on the verge of precipices, on all sides of the valley. I had the pleasure of shaking hands with the chief engineer, a smart man of few words, half-Greek and half-Irish, short and thick set, very dark, a bachelor, a smoker of ciga-rettes and a very well-informed man. His responsibilities are great, and it speaks well for his vigilance and guarded supervision when it is stated that only one instance is on record of an accident, and that was a man falling down over a hundred feet and breaking his leg. He is recovering rapidly in the hospital. Most of the other engineers are graduates of Universities, and appear to be a superior set of men. The resident clergyman is the Rev J S Jones, licensed to the district by the Bishop of St David's, and he is doing very excellent work here. Sunday was formerly a day of rioting–games, fighting and revellings – but a new order of things reigns here now, and Sunday is strictly observed by attendance at the church services. All the engineers set the men a noble example in this. I hope that I may be pardoned when I say that the scene of operations at Elan Valley well repays a visit ere it be submerged. It is reckoned that the whole scheme will have been completed in three years. Hence it will have taken over ten years in construction – over a million pounds per annum.
Yours faithfully,

David Thomas Hughes
March 5, 1900
Curate of Machynlleth

The Opening of the Scheme

By September 1903 the two upper reservoirs were full, and by July 1904 the water had reached the top of the submerged Gareg-ddu dam. On 21 July 1904 the scheme was officially opened by King Edward VII and Queen Alexandra, with the ceremonial turning on of the water supply sending it on its two-day journey to the Frankley reservoir in Birmingham, and with distribution proper beginning in September. Back at the site, by the summer of 1905 the workforce was being reduced as construction work on the scheme was coming to an end. During the winter of 1905 the Caban-coch reservoir was filling up, thus completing the first phase of the plan. The total cost of the first phase had been £5,852,731 (approximately £400 million in 2019).

In early May 1907 a massive auction was held in the Elan Valley, to sell off all surplus materials along with contractor's plant and machinery. The lots ranged from linen, crockery and cutlery, all sorts of hardware items, tools, furniture, buildings (including the huts from the workers' village), railway trucks and carriages, right up to a ten-ton Goliath steam crane, which sold for £140, and a Hunslet saddle tank locomotive, which fetched £400. Some unusual items found in the sale were a music box, a piano, a bagatelle and billiard table with ivory balls and cues, a magic lantern and other games – all probably from the Public Hall in the workers' village.

With the end of the first phase of construction, and the temporary workers' village dismantled and sold off, work began to make a permanent village with houses built of stone for the Corporation's workers employed in the maintenance of the dams, reservoirs and filter beds. This was duly completed in 1909.

DETAILS OF THE COMPLETED DAMS AND RESERVOIRS

Craig-goch dam is 120 feet high and 513 feet long, giving a top water area of 217 acres and a capacity of 2,028 million gallons. The thickness of the dam at the base is 104 feet with 10 feet of foundations, in all requiring 80,000 cubic yards of masonry.

Pen-y-gareg dam is 123 feet high and 528 feet long, giving a top water level of 124 acres and a capacity of 1,332 million gallons. The thickness of the dam at the base is 115 feet with 17 feet of foundations, in all requiring over 90,000 cubic yards of masonry.

Caban-coch dam is 122 feet high and 610 feet long, giving a top water area of 500 acres and a capacity of 7,815 million gallons. The thickness of the dam at the base is 122 feet with 25 feet of foundations, in all requiring 144,800 cubic yards of masonry. As stated, part of the purpose of this dam is to send 27 million gallons per day of compensation water down the river. This flow of compensation water is used to generate power by turbines situated just below the Caban-coch dam, and this is used to power the works.

Halfway up the Caban-coch reservoir, 40 feet below the top water level, is the Gareg-ddu submerged dam, and just upstream of this is the Foel tower where water is drawn off and sent through the filter beds and aqueduct on its journey to Birmingham.

OVERLEAF: Stone-laying ceremony on the Gareg-ddu viaduct in 1900 (*author's collection*)

Prior to this scheme, Birmingham had relied on five streams and six deep wells, providing the city with approximately 18 million gallons of water per day. Now, at the end of the first phase, from the 70 square miles of the gathering grounds of the Elan and Claerwen Valleys, Birmingham was receiving 27 million gallons per day, with the capacity over time and when needed to receive 75 million gallons per day.

THE SECOND PHASE

The second phase of James Mansergh's plan was to be completed as and when required. The foundations of the Dol-y-mynach dam had to be completed during the first phase of construction (as, following the flooding of the Caban-coch reservoir, these foundations would be under water). If completed, this dam would have been 101 feet high and 938 feet wide, the resultant reservoir covering an area of 148 acres and giving a capacity of 1,640 million gallons. Two further dams were earmarked for this second phase: Cil-oerwynt (109 feet high and 1,052 feet wide, giving a top water area of 269 acres and a capacity of 3,100 million gallons), and Pant-y-beddau (98 feet high and 720 feet wide, covering 244 acres and holding 1,900 million gallons).

In the end, the plans were changed and this second phase never turned out as James Mansergh had envisaged. Dol-y-mynach was never completed, and today it is referred to as 'the unfinished dam'. The other two dams in Mansergh's plans were never even started. Instead, thanks to advances in construction techniques, these dams were superseded by one massive concrete dam with rock facing: the Claerwen dam (184 feet high and 1,166 feet long, with the reservoir it holds back being over four miles long and covering 650 acres, with a capacity when full of 10,625 million gallons).

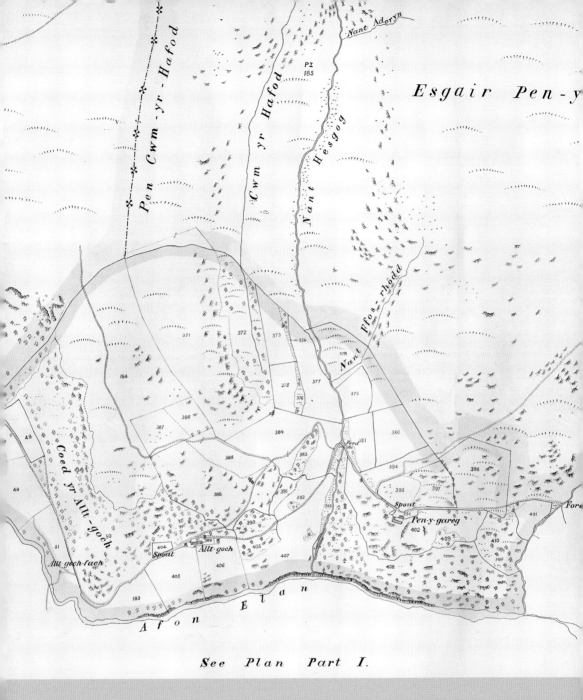

See Plan Part I.

PART **4**

Preparing for the Clearance

☞

Detail of Terrier Plan "L", by surveyor Stephen Williams, 1893, showing a number of the properties in the eastern part of the watershed, including Allt goch-fach which, prior to being submerged under the Pen-y-gareg reservoir, had a short life as the Upper Elan Stores, serving the men and their families employed on the works (see p. 96)

4

WITH THE PASSING of the Birmingham Corporation Water Act 1892 (*outlined in Part Two*) the relevant clauses of the Act now had to be dealt with. One of the main clauses affecting some of the people who lived in the valleys was Clause 14, concerning the displacing of persons of the labouring classes. This clause had to be included in the Act because of another pre-existing Parliamentary Act: namely the Houses of the Working Classes Act 1890. Reports and surveys would now have to be made to determine who would be eligible to be rehoused and which houses needed to be replaced.

During the early part of 1897 a schedule of the houses that came within the scope of the Acts was prepared by Stephen Williams. The schedule included comments and proposals on all of the properties involved, and this included eleven houses in the parish of Llanwrthwl, six of which would be affected by the scheme; and twenty houses in the parish of Llansantffraid Cwmdeuddwr, eight of which would be affected by the scheme.

The following schedule was sent to Mr E.O. Smith, the Town Clerk for Birmingham:

Houses of the Working Classes Act 1890 • Birmingham Corporation Water Act 1892

Schedule of Houses
Parish of Llanwrthwl

1. GRO ISAF

This is a farm house belonging to a farm of the same name but now held by the tenant of Gro Uchaf and the present occupier is therefore a subtenant. He is a carpenter by trade and has no family. If a cottage is built to replace this it will become vacant on the death of the present tenant. [*The tenant, David Jones, who had refused entry to his cottage to allow the Corporation to survey it, had brought lodgers in to live with him since the works had begun, but it would be for him alone that the Corporation would have to provide a replacement cottage. Williams suggested,* 'that to build a large house for one person would be a waste of public money and that in as much as Jones has no family there would no hardship upon him if he were accommodated in part of one of the many other houses in the neighbourhood'. *He also noted,* 'Jones hardly comes under the category of a working man he being partly independent at any rate not always at work.']

A pair of cottages to be built near to the point marked A on the accompanying plan for the accommodation of this and the next following tenant.

NB references throughout to 'A', 'B' etc. apply to a plan whose whereabouts is unknown.

2. Gro Bach

At the time of the passing of the Act this cottage was in the occupation of an old widow named Ann Morgans and I believe she had a daughter living with her immediately on the commencement of the works and they left the neighbourhood and the house became tenanted by the present tenant named Holloway who is occupied on the works. When the works are complete he will no doubt leave the neighbourhood and no house will be required in substitution of this. The obligation to provide such ceased on the original tenant Ann Morgans leaving the neighbourhood.

The proposal for substitution of this and the previous case is based on the assumption that the Local Government Board will require them to be replaced.

One of the proposed cottages to be built at the point A marked on the accompanying plan. See No. 1 above.

3. Penrhiwlan Cottage

The tenant of this cottage (which formerly was a farm house but now for many years held with Llanerchcawr Farm) at the time of the passing of the Act and for some time afterwards was one Thomas Davies who lived there by himself. He was mentally deranged and about the latter end of 1893 or the beginning of 1894 the Poor Law Authorities removed him to the Workhouse where he still remains. [*Following Davies' departure, the cottage was let to workers employed on the scheme, and it was thought that no house would be required to substitute, and if one were built it would remain vacant. Again, the cottage was included due to the assumption that the Local Government Board would require it to be replaced.*]

Cottage to be built attached to the new farmhouse of Llanerchcawr at or near the point marked B on the accompanying plan.

4. Marchnant

The occupier is a shepherd and accommodation must be provided. The present house of Marchnant will not be actually submerged but it will be so near to the edge of one of the reservoirs that it will have to be taken down.

Cottage to be built at or near the point marked C on the accompanying plan.

5. Bryniago Cottage

Occupier is employed on the Elan Estate and it is in order that he may be more conveniently situated for his work on the Estate that this proposed site is fixed upon.

Cottage to be built at or near the point marked D in the parish of Llansantffraid Cwmdeuddwr.

6. Cerig cwplau Cottage

Occupier and his two sons are shepherds so accommodation must be provided.

Cottage to be built at or near the point marked E on the accompanying plan.

7. Pant-tawel Cottage

This house is not included in the proposed scheme submitted to the Local Government Board, and no proposal made to substitute. The cottage will not be interfered with.

No proposal made.

8. Tyn-y-gors Cottage

This house again is outside the limits of the works and will not be interfered with.

No proposal made.

9. Dalrhiw Cottage

The cottage was built in connection with some Lead Mines close at hand and is situated outside the limits of the works. The cottage will not be interfered with but apart from this the Lead Mines are at a standstill and are not likely to be opened again and on completion of works are to be closed. The present tenant will then leave the cottage and quit the neighbourhood and the Corporation will then have the present cottage on hand and it is not likely they will ever be able to relet it.

No proposal made.

10. Llwyndale Cottage

This cottage is let with one of the adjoining farms belonging to the Corporation and at the time of the passing of the Act was occupied solely by a person named John Jones who now has gone to live at Pant-tawel (See No. 7). The cottage will not be interfered with. In the past this cottage has invariably been occupied by persons employed in the mines, and now these are stopped were it not for the works in connection with Birmingham the house would be unoccupied and there is every reason to believe that when the work is completed the house will become vacant.

No proposal made.

11. Pen y gwaith

This is an old house belonging to a disused Lead mine and at the time of the passing of the Act was occupied by a person named Hugh Hughes. He however has left the neighbourhood long ago and the house has been occupied by various persons for short periods since. The house will not be interfered with by the construction of the works and no proposal is made in respect thereof. The house is now quite unnecessary.

No proposal made.

Parish of Llansantffraid Cwmdeuddwr

12. Glan yr afon

Occupier is a road workman and the fixing of the proposed site at F is made owing to its being central for a person superintending the roads in the upper part of the

Elan Valley which is important. Same occupier (Howell Lewis) as at the time of the passing of the Act.

Cottage to be built at or near the point F on the accompanying plan.

13. SHOP-BACH

Tenant is an old widow 80 years of age. She was the sole occupier of the cottage at the time of the passing of the Act. Having regard to the advanced age of this tenant and to the fact that it will be some considerable time before her house will be interfered with it is quite possible that no accommodation be required. Suggest lodgings.

Cottages to be built to replace this and 2 others at or near point marked G on the accompanying plan.

14. TAI-BACH

House was vacant at the time of the passing of the Act. It is submitted that no substitution should be provided and the proposal made is on the assumption that it will be found absolutely necessary to do so.

See above, point marked G.

15. TANYFOEL

Occupier is a tailor and accommodation must be provided. Same occupier (Benjamin Davies) as at time of the passing of the Act.

See above, point marked G.

16. CILOERWYNT FARM HOUSE

This farm was tenanted by a shepherd. He however has now left. This really does not come under the description of workman's dwelling as Ciloerwynt is a farm of very considerable extent and it only happened that it suited the convenience of the previous owner to put a shepherd in that it has been scheduled here at all. When Dolymynach farm will be submerged and also nearly the whole of Ciloerwynt it will be necessary to put up a new farm house at Cwmclyd so as to farm the fringe of these farms that will be left. Submit that this need not be dealt with under the provisions of Act.

A new farm house to be built at point marked H on the accompanying plan.

17. 18. 19. NANTGWILLT COTTAGES

These cottages were occupied by servants of the former owner of the surrounding lands, who on selling to the Corporation left the District taking his servants with him. The cottages are now occupied by Officials of the Corporation who on the completion of the works will leave the neighbourhood and their places taken by Caretakers, for whom houses will be put up at the various dams.

These will be substituted by Caretakers Cottages put up at the various dams.

20. Lluest-torclawdd Cottage

In this case the Corporation under the terms of their arrangement when purchasing this tenement from the previous owners E & D Thomas agreed to grant them 2 acres of ground at a nominal rent of 1/– per annum on which to build their own cottage to replace the one destroyed and this case is therefore disposed of under the terms of the above mentioned arrangement.

No proposal made.

21. Aber calettwr Cottage

This house belongs to a small farm of about 17 acres which has always been sublet with an adjoining farm named Hirnant and was purchased by the Corporation with Hirnant. The name of the tenant at the time of the passing of the Act was Thomas Rowlands who remained up to May 1897 when he left the district.

No proposal made.

22. Aber-y-nant (Seth Thomas)

This is a shop or place of business and always has been so and the tenant is a retired Baptist Minister and clearly does not come within the scope of the Act. The Corporation do not propose to replace this.

No proposal made.

23. Claerwen Cottage

The house is situated entirely outside the limits for works and will not be interfered with in any way and therefore no proposal is made in respect thereof.

No proposal made.

24. Nant y beddau Cottage

This is similar to above and same remarks apply.

No proposal made.

25. Cwmclyd Cottage

This again is a farm house the lands of which have for many years held with an adjoining farm and the house sublet. The house will not however be interfered with. The tenant of the house is William Meredith who was also the tenant at the time of the passing of the Act. He is a miner and until the stoppage of the mines was employed there. He is now employed on the Water Works. He will however in all probability leave the neighbourhood when the works are completed, as he will not be able to obtain any employment. At this point however it is proposed if necessary to build a house in substitution of Ciloerwynt. See No. 16.

No proposal made.

26. Llanerchi Cottage

House belonging to a farm of considerable extent of same name and held with Nantgwillt Farm. The tenant of Llanerchi being a son-in-law of the tenant of Nantgwillt. The house is entirely outside the limits for works and will not be interfered with. At the present time the tenant is engaged on the Water Works but when these are done he will no doubt remain and find employment under his father-in-law on the farms.

No proposal made.

27. Blaencoel Cottage

This house again belongs to a farm of considerable extent of same name and which for many years was held as a by take by the tenant of Cwmcoel Farm. At the time of the passing of the Act the house was vacant as no tenant could be found for it. The Corporations tenant for the tenement is Mr Rees Jones who lives at Cwmcoel Farm who informs me that when his house at Cwmcoel is submerged intends residing at this house. It is outside the limits for works and will not be interfered with.

No proposal made.

28 & 29. Glanrhydwen Cottages   Charles Rees Ann Thomas

These are 2 Cottages on the side of the new line of Railway constructed to connect the works with the Mid Wales Railway. They are situated about 2 ½ miles outside the watershed line and the Railway having been completed no interference will take place.

No proposal made.

30. Llidiart-y-mynydd   Frank Pugh

It is situated outside the limits for works and will not be interfered with and apart from this the Corporation have arranged to grant a lease of the tenement for 31 years to Mr Prickard the former owner, but in fact the conveyance of this property to the Corporation is not yet completed.

No proposal made.

31. Tynyffald

At the time of the passing of the Act the house was unoccupied. No obligation in this case. House outside the limit for works and will not be interfered with.

No proposal made.

(From Powys County Archives R/D/WWA/1/123)

Later, the schedule was reduced to show just the 14 cottages proposed for replacement. The schedule, along with other reports, was sent to the Birmingham Water Committee by Stephen Williams.

In his report, Williams notes,

> I would also point out that in this district labourers cottages are to a great extent unnecessary owing to very little labour being employed on the farms. The work on sheep farms such as all the farms belonging to the Corporation of Birmingham are is chiefly pastoral and very little labour is required. The employment of outside labour is almost unknown and the practice is to have whatever labour is employed, in the shape of indoor servants.

He also added, 'it will be found that several cottages now to be done away with, were then occupied by Widows, who have since died or left the neighbourhood.'

He went on to say,

> as the committee is no doubt aware the majority of the present existing cottages are of a very inferior class, and almost unfit for habitation, and in order to bring this fact fully to the notice of the Officials of the Local Government Board I have had a number of the properties photographed and plans of the interior arrangements prepared so as to give them perfectly accurate and reliable information as to their present condition.

Some of these details appear below:

Particulars of Accommodation and dimensions of Cottages included in Part 1 of the Scheme

Parish of Llanwrthwl in the County of Brecon

1. Gro Isaf
The particulars of this cannot be given owing to the tenant objecting to allow anyone inside the house for the purpose.

2. Gro Bach
This cottage formerly a farm house consists of
Kitchen 16ft 9in x 14ft 6in x 7ft 6in
Larder 10ft x 7ft 7in x 7ft
1 Chamber Bedroom 10ft x 8ft 6in x 7ft
2 Bedroom 18ft 6in x 12ft 9in x 4ft
3 Bedroom 18ft 6in x 13ft 6in x 4ft

3. Penrhiwlan Cottage
This was formerly a farm and the only portion of house and buildings remaining and now occupied as a cottage consists of 2 rooms only
Kitchen 16ft x 13ft 6in x 7ft
Bedroom 16ft x 13ft 6in x 7ft 3in

4. Marchnant Cottage
This was formerly a farm house and consists of
Entrance lobby 6ft x 6ft x 7ft
Kitchen 19ft x 16ft x 7ft

4. Marchnant Cottage (cont.)
Back kitchen 11ft x 11ft x 6ft 7in
Pantry 10ft 6in x 6ft 7in x 6ft 7in
Dairy 10ft x 5ft x 7ft
1 Bedroom 11ft x 10ft 6in x 6ft 3in
2 Bedroom 10ft x 9ft x 6ft 3in
3 Bedroom 20ft x 10ft x 6ft 3in

5. Bryniago Cottage
This cottage consists of
Kitchen 12ft x 12ft x 7ft
Back kitchen 7ft x 5ft 10in x 7ft
Pantry 7ft x 6ft 2in x 7ft
1 Bedroom 12ft x 12ft x 6ft 9in
2 Bedroom 12ft x 12ft x 6ft 9in

6. Cerig Cwplau
This cottage consists of
Kitchen 12ft 6in x 11ft 6in x 7ft
Dairy 11ft 6in x 9ft 6in x 7ft
1 Bedroom 13ft x 12ft x 4ft
2 Bedroom 11ft 6in x 9ft 6in x 4ft

Parish of Llansantffraid Cwmdeuddwr

7. Glanyrafon
This cottage consists of
Passage 17ft x 4ft x 6ft 10in
Kitchen 15ft 6in x 13ft 10in x 7ft
Chamber bedroom 11ft x 6ft 8in x 7ft
1 Bedroom 15ft 6in x 14ft x 4ft 9in
2 Bedroom 10ft x 7ft x 4ft 3in
Lumber room 11ft 6in x 7ft 6in x 6ft

8. Shop bach
This cottage consists of 2 rooms only
Kitchen 10ft 10in x 10ft x 8ft 9in
Bedroom 10ft 6in x 10ft 2in x 8ft 9in

9. Tai bach
This cottage consists of
Kitchen 12ft 6in x 12ft x 7ft 8in
Parlour & passage 12ft 6in x 12ft x 6ft 3in
1 Bedroom 12ft 6in x 10ft x 8ft 6in
2 Bedroom 12ft 6in x 10ft 9in x 8ft 6in

10. Tanyfoel
This cottage consists of
Passage 7ft x 3ft 6in x 7ft
Kitchen 12ft x 12ft x 7ft
Back kitchen 7ft 6in x 8ft 6in x 7ft
1 Bedroom 12ft x 11ft x 5ft 10in
2 Bedroom 12ft x 7ft 6in x 5ft 10in

11. Ciloerwynt
House belonging to a farm
Kitchen 19ft 9in x 18ft 8in x 7ft
Dairy 15ft 4in x 16ft 10in x 8ft
Pantry 5ft 6in x 4ft x 7ft
1 Bedroom 18ft 5in x 20ft x 8ft
2 Bedroom 19ft 6in x 7ft 6in x 5ft
3 Bedroom 19ft 6in x 7ft 6in x 5ft

12. 13 & 14. Nantgwyllt Cottages
The dimensions of these cottages were not
taken as they are at present occupied by
Officials of the Corporation of Birmingham.

Proposed Cottage to be built in Substitution
of those to be destroyed
Entrance lobby 6ft x 5ft x 9ft
Kitchen 15ft x 12ft x 9ft
Back kitchen 15ft x 8ft x 9ft
Pantry 6ft x 10ft x 9ft
1 Bedroom 12ft x 10ft x 7ft 6in
2 Bedroom 9ft x 10ft x 7ft 6in
3 Bedroom 9ft x 10ft x 7ft 6in
4 Bedroom 10ft x 11ft x 7ft 6in

Another report, undated and signed with the initials RWT, detailed the condition of the houses:

Notes

	Artisans Dwellings	Birmingham Water
Walls	Very defective. At "Gro Issaf" shored up in three or four places to prevent collapse. Rear wall of "Shop bach" very damp. Pointing to Walls if any, generally perished, & walls frequently "bulged". Partitions, consist of very rough studding boarded on one side only.	
Roofs	The slating or stone tiles laid only on battens & torched forms the ceiling to the chamber plans, & is not windproof. The roof springs either at the chamber floor level or just above it, so that the average of this floor (storey) would be not more than 4ft 6in. "Glan yr afon" & "Gro bach" are probably less.	
Floors	The ground floors consists of very rough flags. The joists to carry floors over are unceiled & the average height of the ground floor rooms is about 7ft 6in.	
Window openings & ventilation	Totally inadequate as viewed by modern requirements; e.g. "Gro bach" has on the chamber floor not more than 4 sq. ft. of glass; the floor area is 360 sq. ft. and therefore the window space should be 36 sq. ft. (i.e: 360 x 10). "Tai-bach" and "Tan-y-foel" are very similar.	
Stairs	"Pantawel" & "Tai-bach" have only step ladders. At "Gro-bach" it is necessary to use the hands and crawl in order to descend owing to the steepness & narrowness of stairs & lowness of roof.	
Sanitation	Very elementary, an occasional privy. Water has generally to be carried from a distance.	

Notwithstanding this state of things "Gro bach" accommodates eight adult persons. Tan-y-foel accommodates ten adult persons and three children. The tenant of Shop-bach is 82 years old & has lived there for about 50 years and everyone seems to be very healthy. RWT

(From Powys County Archives R/D/WWA/1/123)

Birmingham Town Council submitted copies of the schedules and reports to the Local Government Board which, in May 1897, informed the Birmingham Corporation that a scheme would have to be provided to replace some of the houses which would be lost. A Local Government Enquiry would be held at the Magistrate's Room in Rhayader on 8 February 1898 to consider all proposals.

EXTENT OF PROPOSED FLOODING

Showing the properties affected

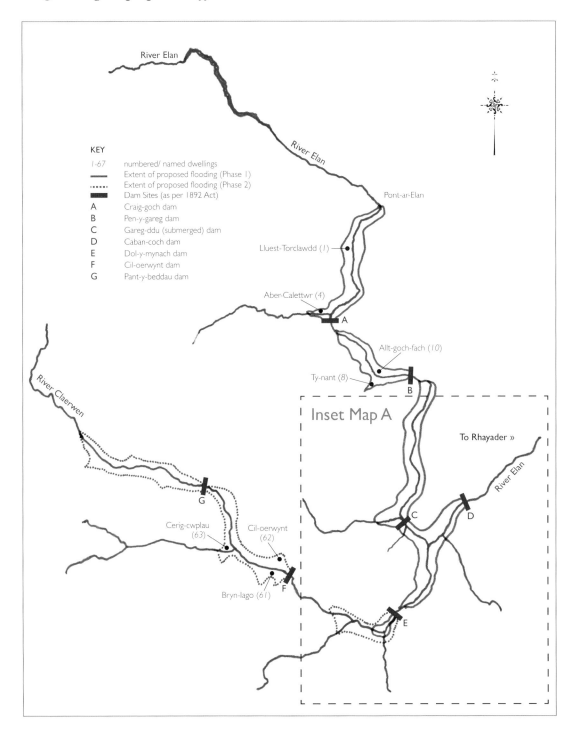

River Elan

River Elan

KEY

1-67 numbered/ named dwellings
— Extent of proposed flooding (Phase 1)
······ Extent of proposed flooding (Phase 2)
▬ Dam Sites (as per 1892 Act)
A Craig-goch dam
B Pen-y-gareg dam
C Gareg-ddu (submerged) dam
D Caban-coch dam
E Dol-y-mynach dam
F Cil-oerwynt dam
G Pant-y-beddau dam

Pont-ar-Elan

Lluest-Torclawdd (*1*)

Aber-Calettwr (*4*)

A

Allt-goch-fach (*10*)

Ty-nant (*8*)

B

River Claerwen

Inset Map A

To Rhayader »

River Elan

C

D

G

Cerig-cwplau (*63*)

Cil-oerwynt (*62*)

Bryn-Iago (*61*)

F

E

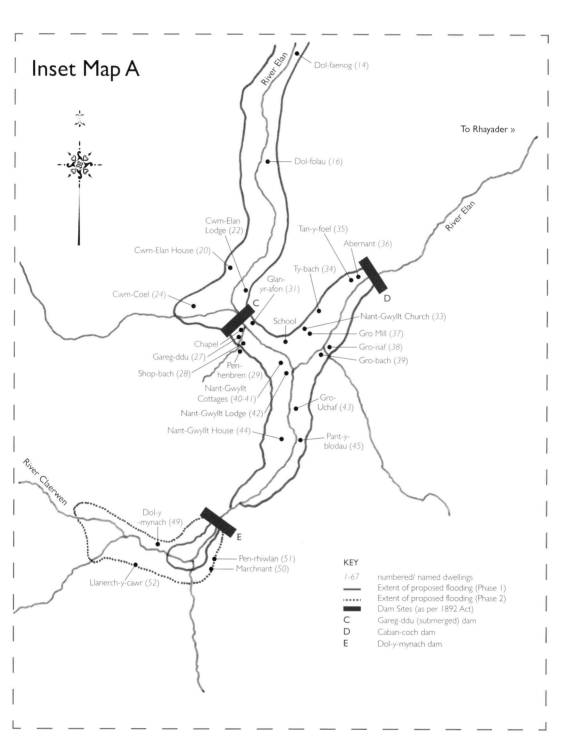

Inset Map A

To Rhayader »

Dol-faenog (14)

River Elan

Dol-folau (16)

River Elan

Cwm-Elan Lodge (22)

Tan-y-foel (35)

Abernant (36)

Cwm-Elan House (20)

Ty-bach (34)

Cwm-Coel (24)

Glan-yr-afon (31)

C

D

School

Nant-Gwyllt Church (33)

Chapel

Gro Mill (37)

Gareg-ddu (27)

Gro-isaf (38)

Pen-henbren (29)

Gro-bach (39)

Shop-bach (28)

Nant-Gwyllt Cottages (40-41)

Nant-Gwyllt Lodge (42)

Gro-Uchaf (43)

Nant-Gwyllt House (44)

Pant-y-blodau (45)

River Claerwen

Dol-y-mynach (49)

E

Pen-rhiwlan (51)

Marchnant (50)

Llanerch-y-cawr (52)

KEY

1-67	numbered/ named dwellings
——	Extent of proposed flooding (Phase 1)
·····	Extent of proposed flooding (Phase 2)
▬	Dam Sites (as per 1892 Act)
C	Gareg-ddu (submerged) dam
D	Caban-coch dam
E	Dol-y-mynach dam

In April 1898, following the enquiry at which Stephen Williams gave evidence on behalf of the Birmingham Corporation, the Local Government Board made it known that only six cottages were required to be rebuilt, fewer than Birmingham had been prepared to replace. The six to be replaced were:

Gro Isaf to be rebuilt at point A
[*above the Nant-y-gro stream and referred to as T'yn-y-pant cottage*]

Marchnant to be rebuilt at point C
[*above T'yn-y-gors and referred to as T'yn-y-gors cottage, Marchnant cottage or New Marchnant*]

Bryniago to be rebuilt at point D
[*next to the abandoned Cwm-Elan Mine and referred to as Cwm-Elan Mine cottage*]

Cerig Cwplau to be rebuilt at point E
[*about a mile further up the Claerwen River at a point where the Nant-y-gader stream enters and referred to as Esgair-y-gader cottage*]

Glanyrafon to be rebuilt at point F
[*close to Pen-y-gareg Farm and referred to as Pen-y-gareg cottage*]

Tanyfoel to be rebuilt at point G
[*opposite the new Baptist Chapel and referred to as Llanfadog cottage*]

NB The locations noted above ('point A', 'point B' etc.) refer to points on a plan which accompanied the Schedule on pp. 73–78; however, during research this plan could not be found.

The sites would be surveyed, plans made and these would be submitted to the Local Government Board for approval. The replacement cottages would consist of a lobby, kitchen, back kitchen, pantry and four bedrooms.

In the minutes of a report to the Water Supply Committee, dated 28 April 1898, it is stated that 'of the above it will only be necessary immediately to substitute the 3 cottages of Gro Isaf, Tanyfoel and Glanyrafon the remaining three are in the valley of the Claerwen and will not be interfered with by the reservoirs now being constructed.'

The Corporation, as well as replacing the church, chapel and school (all of which would be submerged), built the above named cottages in *c.*1900 at a cost of £500 each. All the cottages were roughly of the same design. They were built by local builders, but four of the completed cottages – T'yn-y-gors, Pen-y-gareg, Cwm-Elan Mine and Esgair-y-gader – were deemed by the Corporation to be unfit for habitation, being of poor workmanship and very damp with saturated walls. This was contested by the builders, and various solicitors were involved in resolving the disputes.

Ironically, some of these cottages were never needed due to the later change in plans, and only one of the replacement cottages ever housed the tenant it was intended for.

Some of these cottages are referred to locally as 'Brick House', especially those at Llanfadog and Pen-y-gareg. Four of the cottages still stand today: Pen-y-gareg, Llanfadog and T'yn-y-gors are still let, while Cwm-Elan Mine cottage is in more or less a derelict state. Of the others, T'yn-y-pant was later taken down and Esgair-y-gader disappeared under the later Claerwen reservoir.

A note on Clause 17 of the Birmingham Corporation Water Act ('Leases to present tenants'). In 1895 Edward Wood, the Rhayader solicitor who was acting for a number of tenants, asked for a form of 21-year lease to be provided to his clients under the terms of the 1892 Act, which was duly sent out. Wood had also complained to the Corporation that Stephen Williams was approaching his clients and trying to get them to sign an ordinary estate yearly tenancy instead of the 21-year lease. These clients were named as Mr Jones (Henfron), Rees Jones (Cwm-Coel), Mr Jones (Nant-Gwyllt) and Mr Stephens (Llanerch-y-cawr). In the minutes of a report to the Water Supply Committee, dated 14 October 1895, it was noted that nearly all the tenants had signed agreements; that there were only four outstanding cases that suggested an intention of taking advantage of the 21-year leases, but in all probability would eventually come in as yearly tenants.

There followed several letters between Mr Wood and Mr E.O. Smith (Birmingham Town Clerk) in early 1896, in which Mr Wood claimed that the draft 21-year leases were unfair and not in the spirit of the 1892 Act; and that if the Corporation did not agree to a modification he would advise the tenants to put all the facts before the Welsh Land Commission. After seeking advice, Mr Smith disregarded Mr Wood's observations and stated that Mr Wood's threats would not affect him. He advised that if the tenants were not willing to sign the lease in its present form, but still desired a 21-year lease, then they must settle under the direction of a judge through proceedings between themselves and the Corporation. He also reminded Mr Wood that his clients were at present under notice to quit, pending negotiations and not paying any rent – a situation which could not carry on. After visiting his clients Mr Wood pointed out to Mr Smith that under the Act the tenants were promised leases under the same terms as they had previously held. Mr Wood, having been agent for the previous owners and dealt with many of the farms in question, said that, from his knowledge, the clauses that Mr Wood had deleted from the draft leases were not part of any previous terms and conditions.

Mr Smith must have been getting fed up with his arguments with Mr Wood, as he then wrote to Stephen Williams asking him to visit the tenants in question (as agent for the Corporation) and inform them that unless they signed a 21-year lease in its present form, or an annual tenancy, then steps would be taken to eject them. One by one the first three tenants named above – Mr Jones of Henfron, Rees Jones of Cwm-Coel and Mr Jones of Nant-Gwyllt – came to Stephen Williams and signed a yearly tenancy, and by July 1896 only Mr Stephens of Llanerch-y-cawr had yet to sign. In the minutes of another Water Supply Committee report of 1896 it is noted that Thomas Lloyd Jones of Marchnant had signed his 21-year lease, and therefore only one 21-year lease remained to be granted. Mr Stephens of Llanerch-y-cawr was the one tenant still outstanding who had not signed an agreement – but would later be willing to do so, subject to some slight alterations which had been approved.

Another undated document (probably *c.*1901/2) lists the types of tenancies held, with the majority being annual agreements renewable on Lady Day, the 25 March – the traditional day when tenant farmers renewed or moved on to new farms. The only exceptions in the list are for Marchnant (held under a 21-year lease from 1896) and Lluest-calettwr (held under a 20-year lease from 1899). The properties of Llanerch-y-cawr, Cwm-Coel and Blaen-Coel, although listed as Lady Day annual tenancies, were also subject to the terms and provisions of Clause 17 of the Act, which was the clause that covered 21-year leases – though why this was the case remains unclear.

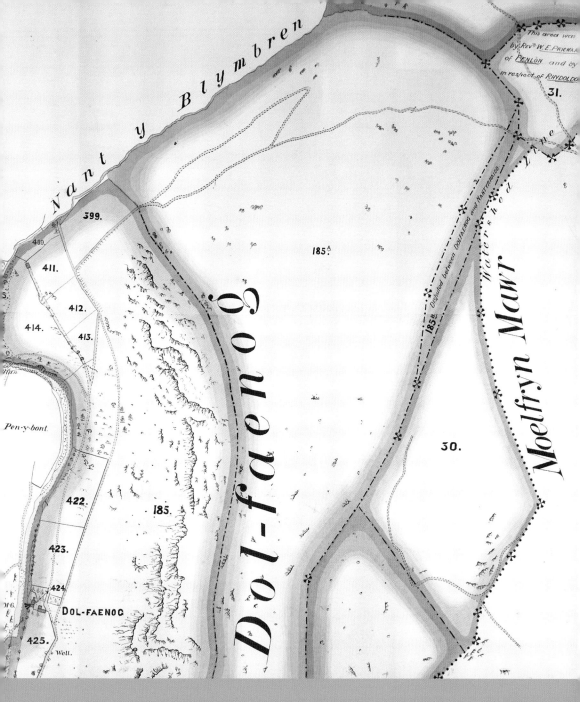

Nant y Blymbren

399.

400.

411.

412.

414.

413.

Pen-y-bont

422.

185.

423.

424.

DOL-FAENOG

425.   Well.

185.ᴬ

Dol-faenog

185.ᴮ Disputed between DOLFAENOG and NANTRIMMIN

Watershed Lane

Moelfryn Mawr

30.

This area was by Revᵈ W. E. PRICHAR of PENLON and by in respect of RHYDOLDO

31.

PART 5

The Fate of the Valleys

☞

Detail of Terrier Plan "M", by surveyor John Jones in c.1894, showing the properties of Pen-y-bont (now home to the newly refurbished tearooms) and Dol-faenog which would be submerged under the upper part of the Caban-coch reservoir. Today this part of the Caban-coch reservoir is referred to as the Gareg-ddu reservoir

5

S o, what happened to all of the inhabitants and their homes situated in the Elan and Claerwen valleys? Over the following pages the properties are looked at one by one; and – using various documents, including censuses, parish registers and electoral rolls – the story is told of what became of the properties and the families who lived in them over the period of the construction of the dams.

The People and Properties of the Elan and Claerwen Valleys 1891–1911

1. Lluest-Torclawdd

This cottage was owned by Edward and David Thomas, and was home to the Price family: David Price (a shepherd); his wife Elizabeth; their four sons, Edward, David, John and Evan; and their five daughters, Elizabeth Jane, Mary Ann, Ellen, Annie and Lucy Jane. In 1891 four of the children were working away from home as servants. Edward was at Glanllyn, closer to the village of Cwmdeuddwr, but the other three were still in the valley: Elizabeth Jane at Allt-goch, David at Pen-y-gareg and Mary Ann at Troed-rhiw-drain. In 1896 daughter Mary Ann died while working away in Nantmel. The rest of the children were also moving about to find work.

By 1901, Edward and David had returned home and were working as labourers, possibly on the works. Elizabeth Jane had moved out to St Harmon where she was employed as a servant. Ellen was working as a housemaid near Llangurig, and John was now boarding at Pen-y-gareg, labouring on the works. Later in 1901 there were two marriages: son Edward married Ellen Morgans at Aberystwyth Register Office, and daughter Ellen married John Davies at Rhayader Register Office, and continued living near Llangurig. In 1903 their son Evan, who had been living at 9 Rock Terrace in Rhayader, died. During the building of the dams, the family (like many others) probably made some extra money by providing tea and Welsh cakes to the workers.

By September 1903 the Craig-goch dam was almost complete and the reservoir had been filled, destroying and submerging Lluest-Torclawdd. It is around this time that the family left the valley. In their agreement with the Corporation, the owners of the property, Edward and David Thomas, had been granted two acres of land on a 999-year lease on which to build a replacement. However, there is no evidence that this was ever done.

The Price family moved to Lluest Pen-rhiw, which was about two miles from Pont-ar-elan on the other side of the mountain road towards Rhayader. Here, David was listed as a farmer. While here, three marriages took place: son David married Mary Elizabeth Davies in 1905; Annie married farmer's son Thomas Price in 1906, and Lucy Jane married John Morgan, a farm labourer from St Harmon two years later. The family remained at Lluest Penr-rhiw until about 1910.

By 1911 David and his wife Elizabeth were living in Castle Row, Rhayader, with David now working as a labourer for the District Council. Of their children, Edward had moved away and was farming in Treharris, Glamorganshire; Elizabeth Jane was still in St Harmon, working as a housekeeper; David was in Rhayader working as a labourer and living just a few doors down from his father; Ellen was living in Llanidloes with her farm contractor husband; Annie was living in the village of Cwmdeuddwr with her husband, who was employed as a waggoner; and Lucy Jane, the youngest daughter, had moved away and was living with her husband, who was a coal haulier in Treharris, not too far away from Lucy's eldest brother Edward.

At times of low water in the reservoir, some remains of Lluest-Torclawdd can still be seen (*see p. 153*).

2. Lluest-cwm-bach

This shepherd's cottage, situated on the Newhouse sheepwalk, was home to the Scott family: Andrew, his wife Sarah and their son John. Although at the time of the 1891 census Andrew was working away at Newhouse farm in Cwmdeuddwr, by the time of Stephen Williams' census in 1892 he had returned, and there had also been the addition of another son, George. The property would not be affected by the scheme, and although some of the access paths to it would end up under water, the cottage remained and was home to members of the Scott family for many years thereafter.

Andrew and Sarah would have another son, William in 1894. By 1901 their eldest son John was working as a crane stoker on the works, and George was boarding down at Park Farm near Cwmdeuddwr. Andrew died in 1903 and, following this, John probably took over the shepherding. In 1908 he married, and by 1911 he is listed as shepherd at Lluest-cwm-bach, along with his wife Mary Ann and his younger brother William who was also shepherding. Sarah and son George were living in the newly-built Elan Village where George was employed by the Corporation as a carpenter. Much later, Lluest-cwm-bach would become abandoned, but it has now been renovated and today it is used as a walker's bothy.

3. Hirnant

This farmhouse is another property that would not be affected by the works. It was home to farmer John Thomas and his wife Anne, along with their nephew John Lewis Pugh, who was a shepherd. Although Hirnant was unaffected by the works, by 1901 the three occupants had moved to the farm Wernhir near the village of Llanyre, just a few miles south of Rhayader. The electoral rolls show that John must still have had the tenancy of Hirnant up to about 1902, the year he died, as he is listed under both addresses (he may have sublet Hirnant during this time). Anne remained at Wernhir until her death in 1917, while John Lewis Pugh married in 1906 and continued to farm Wernhir for many years thereafter.

In 1901 Hirnant was home to a shepherd, David Jones, and by 1906 shepherd James Worthing had taken over. Although Hirnant has been rebuilt, the farm still exists to this day.

4. Aber-Calettwr

This cottage was home to farmer and shepherd Thomas Rowlands and his wife Sarah. According to Stephen Williams, Thomas and Sarah left Aber-Calettwr in 1897, moving to the eastern part of Radnorshire, to a farm by the name of Lower Voel in Beguildy. However, by 1911 they were back living locally in the parish of Llanwrthwl with Sarah's brothers William and John Hughes at a farm called Pistyllgwyn. Here, Thomas was assisting the Hughes brothers (formerly of Allt-goch), and Sarah was housekeeping for them. Soon after, Thomas and Sarah would move to Penwain in Nantmel.

After the Rowlands had left, an incomer to the valley, by the name of John Morgans, occupied Aber-Calettwr for a short while before the cottage was demolished. There is an interesting account of his eviction (unfortunately undated and unsigned).

<u>Birmingham Corporation</u>
<u>Elan Estate</u>
<u>Aber calettwr House</u>

In pursuance of instructions I yesterday accompanied the County Court Bailiff to Aber calettwr to receive from him possession of the house. When we arrived there the tenant John Morgans was in possession and refused to quit. There were also present the Corporation Estate Workmen and a Police Constable. On the Bailiff commencing to remove the furniture some opposition was shewn by Morgans but on the interference of the Constable the removal of the furniture was continued and completed. After the furniture was all out of the house I ordered the Estate Workmen to take off the roof. This was done and all the material of any value was stored on one side. All the roof timbers were taken off and partitions inside cleared away. As the work of demolishing the whole structure was drawing to a close the tenant's son George Morgans arrived on the scene and commenced assaulting the workmen. His conduct became so disorderly that the Constable had to interfere and a good deal of scuffling took place, on being released by the Constable, Morgans although he promised to conduct himself rushed towards the house and commenced smashing the windows and with an axe broke down the door and proceeded to commit other damage to the old material taken out of the house. I did not deem prudent to having regard to all the circumstances to charge him with wilful damage to property and have him locked up, for the reason that the cost of prosecuting him in all probability [would] exceed the damage he would commit apart from the odium that would arise from the Corporation appearing as prosecutors. The roof and main timbers having been taken away, nothing much remains but the main walls, but it is not improbable that Morgans will attempt for a time to squat there and utilize the old material to put up a shelter for himself. Possession having now been obtained the Works Department should at once see that the walls of the old house are taken down and the place cleared, and thus avoid the possibility of the Corporation having again to bring an action of ejectment to get rid of him off the ground.

Transcribed from Powys County Archives R/D/WWA/1/15

5. Lluest-aber-caethon

This shepherd's cottage was situated above Aber-Calettwr and well away from the works, so was left untouched. Mary Powell lived here along with her son, John Robert; her daughter, Mary Ann; her grandson, John Powell Owens, and a servant by the name of Andrew Price who came from Knighton and had formerly been in the workhouse there.

The family shepherded for the tenant of Abercaethon Farm, which was closer to the village of Cwmdeuddwr. In around 1894, the tenant of Abercaethon Farm died and the Powell family took over the tenancy and moved there, but they continued to use Lluest-aber-caethon as a shelter when they were engaged in looking after the sheep. Mary Powell died in 1899, and by 1901 Mary's children, John Robert and Mary Ann, were farming Abercaethon (the family remained there for some time thereafter).

In 1900 John Powell Owens was married, and in 1901 he was shepherding at Lluest-calettwr along with his wife. In 1899 the Corporation had leased Lluest-calettwr to John Robert Powell for 20 years, so this would account for why John Powell Owens, who was his nephew, was shepherding there for him. However, by 1911 he had joined his uncle at Abercaethon. In 1911 Lluest-aber-caethon was occupied by another shepherd, by the name of George Morgans – the same George Morgans mentioned in the account above about Aber-Calettwr (when his father John Morgans was evicted). Lluest-aber-caethon still stands today, but is in ruins.

The ruins of Lluest-aber-caethon (5) today

6. Lluest-calettwr

This cottage was even further away from the works than the previous property, and was unoccupied in 1891. In 1898 it was surveyed. The house was said to be in a dilapidated state but the outbuildings were in better condition and still being used as cattle sheds. In the report it noted that John Robert Powell had given notice of his intention to obtain a lease under section 17 of the Act, and it was suggested if he did that he should carry out repairs. As previously mentioned, it was leased to the above Powell family in 1899 for 20 years, and occupied in 1901. However, by 1911 it was unoccupied again, and probably just being used as shelter for the shepherd. It later became abandoned.

7. Llanerch-lleyn

This was farmed by Elizabeth Davies and her two sons, Henry and Edward, along with a domestic servant, Mary Morgan. They were an all Welsh-speaking family. Elizabeth died in 1892, so her sons carried on at the farm, and in 1895 Edward married their servant Mary Morgan. Although the farmhouse itself would not be affected, the rent of the property was reduced due to land being taken for the works. In 1900, in a tragic accident, Edward drowned in the River Elan. As a result, by 1901, his wife Mary was running the farm, accompanied by two young children and her brother-in-law Henry who was now listed as being retired. Mary had also employed a shepherd by the name of Thomas Lewis, and in that same year the two were married. Soon after, they left Llanerch-lleyn, and by 1911 they were farming at Cefngilfach in Abergwesyn, Breconshire.

Henry also moved out around the same time, and it is believed he lodged at T'yn-y-pant cottage, one of the newly-built replacement cottages, where he died in 1910.

Llanerch-lleyn would end up being situated right on the edge of the Pen-y-gareg reservoir. It was attached to the neighbouring farm Ty-nant, and it appears to have been occupied by Edward Morgan in 1904–05; however, by 1906 the land had become part of Abercaethon farm which belonged to the Powell family, and Llanerch-lleyn farmhouse was no longer used and became abandoned. Today a few walls can still be seen (*see p. 154*).

8. Ty-nant

A cottage occupied by the Morgan family: David and his wife Anne, and their son and daughter, Edward and Elizabeth Ann. They also had two servants from elsewhere in the valley: David Price from Gareg-ddu, and Jane Lawrence from Pen-cae-haidd.

During the building of the dams the farm received the sum of £8 in compensation and had its rent reduced for land taken. In 1899 Anne died, followed by her husband David in 1902. David had been a long-serving deacon of the Bethania Chapel in the valley. Shortly after this the family must have left Ty-nant, with Edward moving to nearby Llanerch-lleyn in 1904; however, by 1911 it appears that he had moved away to Nantmel where he was farming at Penlan.

Elizabeth Ann also moved out in about 1904 and went to live at Pen-y-bont, which was part of the Ty-nant holding. While living there she married David Griffiths from Shop-bach in 1908. By 1911 they had moved away to Newbridge-on-Wye where David had found work as a labourer on an estate.

Ty-nant would be submerged under the Pen-y-gareg reservoir, and some of the remaining land became attached to Abercaethon farm. At very low water some walls of Ty-nant become visible (*see p. 156*).

9. Troed-rhiw-drain

This farm was well away from the rising waters, and would not be interfered with. It was farmed by the Williams family: David and Mary, their daughter Mary, son David and a grandson, William Walter Williams. They also employed a local girl, Mary Ann Price, as a domestic servant.

The family remained at the farm throughout. Daughter Mary died in 1892, and son David married Sarah Jones from the Henfron in 1895. By 1911 both parents, David and Mary, had died, leaving son David and his family running the farm. William Walter was working for his uncle as a shepherd.

Troed-rhiw-drain still exists today.

TOP: Allt-goch-fach (10) in 1892 (*by permission of the Library of Birmingham MS944 BCC ST 2008/214/Box 45*). BOTTOM: the same scene of Allt-goch-fach (10) in 2018

Allt-goch-fach (10) in its short life as the Upper Elan Stores (Richard Hughes Collection)

10. ALLT-GOCH-FACH

This belonged to the farm of Allt-goch and was unoccupied in 1891. By 1901 it was occupied by a worker employed on the scheme, and a wooden extension had been attached to the cottage which, between 1897 and 1904, became the Upper Elan Stores. When the property was flooded by the Pen-y-gareg reservoir, this wooden extension floated away. It was retrieved and later became a mission hut on the side of the reservoir.

11. ALLT-GOCH

Allt-goch was home to widow Sarah Hughes and her two sons, William and John, who farmed here. They also employed two servants from elsewhere in the valley: Elizabeth Price from Lluest-Torclawdd and Howell Lewis from Glan-yr-afon. Although the farm would remain, it would be significantly reduced in size owing to the land taken by the Corporation, mainly for the construction of the railway. In 1896 the family received the sum of £12 in compensation, and the rent was reduced from £60 per annum to £35. In 1903 Sarah died, leaving William and John running the farm.

After Sarah's death, William and John left the farm and moved to the neighbouring parish of Llanwrthwl, initially to farm at the Van before moving to Pistyllgwyn close by. Allt-goch would be taken over by the Evans family from Dol-faenog, a property a little further down the valley, which would be flooded.

Allt-goch still exists today, although it has been rebuilt.

12. PEN-Y-GAREG

Pen-y-gareg farm was in a similar situation to Allt-goch. The farm would remain and would lose some of its land to the works, for which the family received £11 in compensation and a reduction in rent. In 1891 it was farmed by David Evans. His niece Anne Evans kept house for him, and there were three servants (two from elsewhere in the valley): Edward Price from Gareg-ddu and David Price from Lluest-Torclawdd; the other being a Mary Anne Evans.

David and Anne remained at the farm throughout this period, and by 1901 they had a number of labourers employed on the works lodging with them. In 1902 a yearly agreement was signed by David Evans for the tenancy of the farm, and in 1911 David had been joined by a nephew and his family to help on the farm.

Pen-y-gareg has also been altered but still exists today.

13. PEN-Y-BONT

As previously mentioned, this came under the same holding as Ty-nant (8). It was unoccupied in 1891, and housed workers in 1901. However, once the Morgan family had left Ty-nant in around 1904 some members of the family continued to live at Pen-y-bont until about 1910 when the property became vacant again.

At the time of the 1911 census Pen-y-bont cottage is recorded as having building work being done. It became a much bigger property, and at one time was home to the Corporation Estate Agent, John Jones.

After further tenants it later became tearooms and a B&B which closed a couple of years ago. However, after further alterations it reopened again in 2019.

14. DOL-FAENOG

Dol-faenog (*visible in the centre of the picture overleaf, p. 98*), was home to another Evans family: shepherd Edward Evans, his wife Martha, their daughter Mary Anne and grandson Edward James.

Although Dol-faenog would be submerged, the family continued here until that time came. In 1896 they received £10 compensation and had their rent reduced for land taken for the works while they continued to farm. In 1898 daughter Mary Anne married John Evans (who appears to have been employed on the works as a platelayer), and in 1901 he was living with the family at Dol-faenog. As noted above, when the family had to leave their home they all moved to Allt-goch, to take over from the Hughes family.

TOP: Between Pen-y-bont and Cwm-Elan in 1895, showing Dol-faenog (14) next to the river, the works railway already having been laid (*by permission of the Library of Birmingham MS944/114/16*). BOTTOM: the same scene from a similar viewpoint in 2018

Edward died in 1904 and his wife Martha in 1907. Their daughter Mary Anne and her husband continued at Allt-goch, and in 1911 they had four children and a servant living with them. The family continued to farm at Allt-goch for many years thereafter.

Grandson Edward James Evans also worked as a shepherd at Dol-faenog, and presumably moved with the family to Allt-goch. However, by 1911 he had moved down to Mountain Ash in Glamorganshire where he was working as a miner.

15. Ty'n-y-llidiart

This farm would not be affected by the works. It was farmed by William Ingram and his wife Jane, along with a farm servant, David Griffiths from Shop-bach. The property appeared in a special report (compiled by Stephen Williams and dated 13 June 1898) on the farms the Corporation had just purchased from the Dderw Estate, and in which was outlined the state of the houses and buildings, and the repairs required. Williams made the point that, 'The former owners (Mr Prickard's Trustees) having regard to the fact that the Corporation would eventually be compelled to purchase this property were reluctant or unwilling to carry out even necessary repairs and as a consequence matters have for the last 6 or 7 years been rapidly going from bad to worse'. Ty'n-y-llidiart was described as a farmhouse consisting of kitchen, dairy and chamber bedroom on the ground floor with three bedrooms above. The roof was in a very bad state with many tiles having blown away and the laths perished, along with one gable end wall tumbling down. Williams said, 'As at present I have no hesitation in saying that if the house were visited by a sanitary officer, it would be condemned as utterly unfit for habitation, and something must be done at once'. His proposals for repairs recommended that the roof and timbers should be replaced, gable end wall rebuilt, kitchen floor tiled, new windows, doors and the baking oven repaired. There was no fire grate in the house, as turf was used as fuel instead of coal, and Williams stated in his report, 'The tenant is willing and indeed would prefer to continue to have his fire on the hearth stone in the old fashioned and primitive way with baking and cooking done in iron pots covered with burning turf and hot ashes'. In total Stephen Williams' estimate for repairs to the house and outbuildings was £85. By 1901 William and Jane were still farming there, but with a change of farm servant. In 1911 William, now aged 83 and listed as a retired farmer, had been joined by a nephew to help run the farm. William died later that year.

Today Ty'n-y-llidiart is let as a holiday cottage.

16. Dol-folau

A large family by the name of Morgans lived at Dol-folau. The family consisted of farmer Thomas and his wife Mary along with six sons, Thomas Richard, Evan Price, Edward Arthur, Richard Charles, William Alfred, David Ivor; and three daughters, Mary Ann, Elizabeth and Eveline.

Dol-folau would be lost to the reservoir, but the family continued farming until it was time to vacate the property. In 1894 Thomas's wife Mary died at the age of 45. Like other farms, Dol-folau also lost some of its land to the works prior to flooding, and the family received compensation for this.

In 1900 the eldest daughter Mary Ann married David Joseph Davies, a driller on the works who had been housed just across the river at Ty'n-y-ffald. By 1901 they were living at Pen-y-bont where David was listed as a mason's labourer. After the works finished, Mary Ann and her husband moved to Merthyr Tydfil where he worked as a colliery fireman. They named their home there 'Dolfolau House' and stayed there for the rest of their lives – but were brought back to be buried in Cwmdeuddwr churchyard. Of the other children who moved away before 1901, the eldest son, Thomas Richard, was employed by the Corporation. In 1901 he was living in Bewdley, Worcestershire and employed as a chainman. Later that year he married Annie Hardwick in Kidderminster. By 1911 he had moved back closer to home to live at Clywedog cottage near Penybont Station with his wife and son, where he was employed as a waterworks walksman by the Corporation. Elizabeth also left home before 1901, and went to Aberedw just south of Builth Wells, where she was employed as cook for a local ironmonger. In 1903 she married blacksmith Arthur Norman, and by 1911 they had moved to Talgarth.

All the rest of the children, along with father Thomas, were still working Dol-folau in 1901. Son Evan had married Selina James in Worcester in 1900, which may suggest that Evan, too, briefly worked for the Corporation like his elder brother; however, by 1901 he had returned to Dol-folau with his wife. Evan and Selina went on to have three children before they left the valley. The last of these, Gertrude Jane, was born in December 1903; the Corporation allowing the baby to be born at Dol-folau before they had to quit the property. Gertrude Jane must surely have been the last baby to be born in the soon-to-be-flooded valley to a family which had to leave their home.

So, in 1904 the family left Dol-folau. In 1908 father Thomas remarried, and by 1911 he was farming at Blaenglyn in Llangurig, along with his youngest son David Ivor. Evan Price Morgans and his wife Selina moved to Church Street in Rhayader, from where Evan worked as a quarry labourer. Eveline Morgans also moved to Rhayader, living at Kendal House where she was listed as a shopkeeper. Edward Arthur married in 1905, and by 1911 he and his wife Ellen were farming at Pen-caeau in the parish of Cwmdeuddwr, close to the Dderw Estate. William Alfred found work at Aber-gwngu farm (in the upper reaches of the Elan, but still within the Corporation's watershed).

As for Richard Charles Morgans, he moved down to South Wales, married Winifred Bennett and settled in Mountain Ash where he worked as a miner.

17. Cringwm

This was unoccupied in 1891, and in 1898 it was included in the report produced by Stephen Williams on the Dderw Estate properties purchased by the Corporation. In that report it stated, 'The house until of late years was in a fairly good state of repair and occupied by a shepherd. Of recent years it has become untenanted and neglected'. It remained unoccupied and became abandoned.

TOP: The ruins of Cringwm (17) in 2015. BOTTOM: The ruins of T'yn-y-ffald (18) in 2015

18. Ty'n-y-ffald

This property was also uninhabited in 1891. It was said to be in not too bad a state, as a previous tenant had done some repairs. During the building of the dams and reservoirs it housed workers, but by 1911 it was empty again and was eventually abandoned.

19. Llanerch-ty-newydd

Part of the Henfron holding, this property was in a poor state of repair and remained unoccupied throughout, becoming abandoned (*see p. 160*).

20. Cwm-Elan House

This house was owned by Robert Lewis Lloyd, but he did not use it as his main residence. The house's claim to fame had been through one of its previous owners, Thomas Grove, the uncle of the poet Percy Shelley, who visited the property.

In 1891 the property was home to Edward Davies, a gardener; his wife and daughter (who were both named Fanny and were both housekeepers), and servant Catherine Lloyd from Nant-Gwyllt Lodge. The other occupants of the house were three civil engineers (Seymour William Williams, Sydney Cooke Lewis and Richard Eustace Tickell), which reflects that work was already beginning on the scheme by this date.

Edward Davies died in 1893, and his wife and daughter stayed on as housekeepers, probably until the house was due to be flooded. By 1901 it still housed civil engineers (although not the same ones), and there was now a housemaid and parlour maid.

After Cwm-Elan House was flooded, Fanny and her daughter moved to The Firs in Rhayader where they ran a boarding house. Mother Fanny died there in 1909, her daughter carrying on as boarding house keeper.

Cwm-Elan House (20) in 1897 (*by permission of Powys Archives R/D/CL/1/27*)

TOP: The stables and farm buildings of Cwm-Elan House (*by permission of Powys Archives R/D/CL/1/40*). BOTTOM: the same scene viewed from the Elan Valley Trail in 2014

TOP: Cwm-Elan House (20) in 1895 (the Cwm-Elan Mine was situated in the valley above the house) (*by permission of Powys Archives R/D/CL/1/28*). BOTTOM: the same scene in 2018

Some of the ruins of Cwm-Elan Mine (21), together with one of the replacement cottages

21. CWM-ELAN MINE

Up above Cwm-Elan House was the mine with all of its associated buildings. The property was unoccupied in 1891, the mine abandoned and no longer working. One of the replacement cottages was built next to the old mine house, and in 1901 this housed 11 workers. By 1911 the cottage was home to a gamekeeper on the estate (an incomer to the valley employed by the Corporation).

Remains of the old mine buildings together with the replacement cottage, which is now in a poor state of repair, can still be seen today.

22. CWM-ELAN LODGE

Situated on the opposite bank of the river to the main house, the lodge was occupied in 1891 by the widow Anne Davies who had formerly lived at Cwm-Coel. By 1901 Anne had moved out and was boarding at Park Farm nearer to Cwmdeuddwr, where she died shortly after. In 1901 the lodge had been taken over by a woodman and his family. The lodge would be flooded by the reservoir.

23. HENFRON

Henfron, apart from losing some of its access roads to the rising waters, would remain untouched by the works. It was home to farmer John Jones, his wife Margaret, their son William, and daughters Sarah and Mary, along with a farm servant, James Jones.

The Jones family outside Henfron, *from left to right:* James Jones (farm servant), John and Margaret Jones, daughters Mary and Sarah, and son William Jones (*Betty Davies Collection*)

As noted previously, daughter Sarah married David Williams from Troed-rhiw-drain in 1895, and she made her home there with her husband. In 1900 the other daughter, Mary, married John Price from Nant-y-beddau in the Claerwen valley, and she went to live there. This was the last wedding to take place in the old Nant-Gwyllt Church which was to be flooded by the Caban-coch reservoir. By 1901 some grandchildren had come to live at the farm, and the family had also taken in a lodger. In 1910 Margaret died, and the following year daughter Mary died. In 1911 John was listed as a retired farmer and William had taken over. The grandchildren were still at the farm, along with a servant and a shepherd, and they also had a gamekeeper lodging at the farm.

Farm servant James Jones married Annie Meredith from the nearby farm Pen-glan-Einon in 1891, and they soon moved away from the valley down to Mountain Ash in Glamorganshire, where James took a job as a miner. However, by 1918 they had returned to Pen-glan-Einon, and their son, also James, would go on to live in one of the Corporation's replacement cottages close to the Pen-y-gareg dam.

Henfron is still a working farm today.

24. Cwm-Coel

Another large family resided at Cwm-Coel: farmer Rees Jones and his wife Anne; their seven daughters: Mary Ann, Sarah Alice, Ruth, Margaretta Jane, Magdalene Flora, Beatrice and Anne; and their two sons: John and Thomas Lloyd, together with a cowman, Thomas Hamer.

Rees received the sum of £7 10s for land taken for the works during the time the family continued to farm at Cwm-Coel. In 1894 there was an addition to the family, with the arrival of another daughter, named Olwen Gertrude Amy. Then, in 1899 the eldest daughter Mary Ann married Owen George Bowen, a carpenter from Newtown. A year later, in 1900, son John married Catherine Williams from Dol-y-mynach Farm in the Claerwen valley. This was the first wedding to take place in the new Nant-Gwyllt Church, built by the Corporation to replace the old one which was to be submerged. By 1901 Mary Ann had moved away with her new husband to live in Ashford, Middlesex, and Beatrice was working as a housemaid at Ffrondorddu in Llanwrthwl. The rest of the family, along with some additions, were still at the farm and there had been a change of farm servant. As well as the compensation and rent reduction, the Corporation allowed a hut to be built at Cwm-Coel, and at this time eight workers were lodging there. Later in 1901 Sarah Alice married Frederick William Boys, a Danish man employed as a cashier on the works. After the completion of the dams they went to live in Washford, Somerset, where Frederick was employed as a clerk in a mine works.

The next three daughters also married, and all ended up moving away and living in Glyncorrwg, Glamorganshire. In 1903 Margaretta Jane married Arthur Henry Jones, a mason on the works from Bristol. In 1906 Magdalene Flora married Edward Gilbert, an engine driver from Glyncorrwg, and in the same year Ruth married a local farmer, John Edwards (strangely this marriage took place in London). By 1911 all three girls were living on the same street in Glyncorrwg, Ruth and Margaretta being next-door neighbours. Interestingly, Magdalene had called her home 'Rhayader House' and Margaretta's was named 'Cwmcoel'. Ruth would later return home with her husband and family to farm at Tyn-castell in Llanwrthwl.

Back at home, around 1903, the family had to leave Cwm-Coel, as this was soon to be flooded. As recorded in the survey undertaken by the Corporation in 1898, Rees gave the impression that after Cwm-Coel was flooded he would live at Blaen-Coel, a property further up the Cwm-Coel stream and already part of the tenancy, and Rees would have been eligible for a 21-year lease. However, for some reason Rees did not take up this option and the family instead left the valley. By 1911 the family had moved closer to the village of Cwmdeuddwr where they were to farm at Coedmynach, a farm also owned by Robert Lewis Lloyd. Also at Coedmynach were wife Anne, daughters Beatrice and Olwen Gertrude, and son Thomas Lloyd, along with a grandson, William Henry Jones, and a servant. The family went on to farm at Coedmynach for many years thereafter. It is possible that, although he and his family moved to Coedmynach, Rees could have retained the tenancy on the land at Cwm-Coel.

In around 1906 son John, his wife Catherine and their family had moved to Dyffryn farm in the parish of Nantmel. In 1911 John's sister Anne was also at the farm helping to nurse John and Catherine's newborn baby.

25. Blaen-Coel

Blaen-Coel would not be affected by the works. Living there in 1891 were William Roberts, a lead miner, together with his wife Margaret, their son John Thomas and daughter Effie Anne.

Although unaffected, by 1901 the family had left the valley and moved to the neighbouring parish of Llanwrthwl where, for many years, they farmed at Erwllwyn.

In 1901 Blaen-Coel was uninhabited, and in 1911 it was home to Daniel Price, a shepherd from Nant-y-beddau in the Claerwen valley. It later became abandoned and today lies in ruins.

26. Baptist Chapel and cottage

Adjacent to the Baptist Chapel was a cottage. This was home to Christopher Price, listed in 1891 as living on parish relief. He died the following year and was one of the last people to be buried in the Baptist Chapel graveyard.

Baptist Chapel Cottage (26)

The chapel, cottage and graveyard would all be submerged under the Caban-coch reservoir. The chapel had been leased to the Trustees in 1846 for 999 years; the residue of the lease being assigned to the Corporation by the Trustees in exchange for a new piece of land and the building of a new chapel. This was built just beyond the Caban-coch dam site, near Llanfadog. Those buried in the graveyard were removed and reinterred in the graveyard at the newly built chapel. The Corporation would pay an allowance of £10 per grave. In a letter dated 14 May 1896, there is an account of the removal of the remains of five of the relatives of a W. Richard Lloyd, formerly of Gareg-ddu and subsequently of Porth, Glamorganshire. Mr Lloyd had come to supervise the removal, disinterment and reinterment, all of which was carried out by the Corporation at their expense. The conveyance of the bodies from the old to the new graveyard, together with the coffins, was paid for by Mr Lloyd at a cost of £12 14s 10d. This cost was submitted to the Corporation and in due course settled by them to Mr Lloyd's solicitors.

27. Gareg-ddu

This was home to farmer, Rees Price, his wife Mary and son Thomas. They also had two sons working elsewhere in the valley: Edward Rees Price at Pen-y-gareg and David Price at Ty-nant. Like other affected farmers, Rees received £5 in compensation, as almost all of his land was taken for the works, and his rent was reduced. In 1897 Edward Rees Price married Margaret Ann Hughes, and the following year his father Rees died. Son David Price, having now returned home from Ty-nant, married Caroline James in 1900. She had come to the valley from Herefordshire probably with her family to find work, and it appears that she had been employed at one of the engineers' houses in the valley as a housemaid. At this time, David was employed as a coachman, probably by the Corporation.

By 1901, still at Gareg-ddu were Mary, her two sons, Thomas and David, David's wife Caroline, a grandson and two lodgers who were lead miners. The remaining son, Edward was by now living at Pen-y-gwaith in the Claerwen valley with his wife Margaret, where he too was working as a lead miner.

Gareg-ddu would be flooded by the Caban-coch reservoir, so the family would have to leave. By 1911 Mary was living at Crownant cottage in Rhayader, and Edward Rees Price and his family were living at Ty'n-y-pant (one of the replacement cottages built by the Corporation in the Parish of Llanwrthwl), Edward having now been employed by the Corporation as a labourer. David and his family moved down to South Wales to live in Treherbert, where David was a coal miner. Thomas also moved to South Wales, married Elizabeth Marks in 1910 and settled in Aberdare where he worked as a colliery labourer. In 1914 Edward Rees Price also left the area and moved to South Wales where he too became a miner.

28. SHOP-BACH

This was a small cottage of two rooms (each roughly ten-feet square with a couple of tiny two-foot square windows) in which, in 1891, Anne Griffiths lived with her grand-daughter Emmeline. She also had a son, David, working elsewhere in the valley at Ty'n-y-llidiart.

In 1896 Emmeline married a lead miner, George Morgan, and they went to live at Llwyn-dale, an old miner's cottage in the Rhiwnant valley. By 1901 David had returned to live at Shop-bach, and was now listed as a general labourer, so possibly had found employment on the works. There was also a grandson living at the cottage.

With the demolition of this property, the family moved out around 1904. Anne, her daughter Emmeline and her husband moved down to Glamorganshire where they lived in Llwynpia. Emmeline's husband was employed as a stoker in a colliery there. In 1907 Anne died and was buried back home in Cwmdeuddwr churchyard. David married Elizabeth Ann Morgan, formerly of Ty-nant, in 1908 and by 1911 they were living in Newbridge-on-Wye where David was employed as an estate labourer.

29. PEN-HENBREN

Although this farm would not be flooded, it would be demolished to make way for the new road, which would go right through the property.

Pen-henbren (29) (*foreground*), was demolished to make way for the new road which would lead off from the Gareg-ddu viaduct. Also visible in the distance is Cwm-Elan House, on the edge of the rising waters (*Betty Davies Collection*)

Pen-henbren was home to farmer Evan Price, his wife Margaret, their daughter Elizabeth and their grandson David. They also had a lodger, Thomas Jones, who was employed as a carpenter. Like other farms, they lost land during the construction works, and for the road diversion they received the sum of £1 in compensation. In 1894 grandson David died at the age of 13, and in 1897 Evan passed away. The following year, daughter Elizabeth married Robert Roberts, a labourer on the works. Thus, by 1901 Pen-henbren was occupied by Robert Roberts (now employed as a stationary engine driver), his wife Elizabeth, her mother Margaret and a sister, Mary, who had returned home from working away in service. They also housed three lodgers, all of whom were employed on the works. In April 1901 Margaret died, and later in October daughter Mary married John Thomas Williams from Cil-oerwynt in the Claerwen valley, and she moved there to farm with her husband.

The family stayed at Pen-henbren until around 1905; however, by 1911, with the farm now demolished, Robert and his wife had moved to live in Cambrian Terrace, Rhayader, where Robert was employed as a labourer for the Council.

30. Llanerchi

Shepherd Thomas Davies lived here with his wife Sarah Ann, their four sons, Evan, John Pryce, David and Albert Edward; and three daughters, Mary Ann, Margaret and Sarah. There were also a further two sons, Thomas and William Walter, who were working away from home in the Claerwen valley for their grandfather, Evan Jones at Pant-y-blodau.

The year 1897 saw the death of William Walter Davies, aged 22; while at Pant-y-blodau, the following year, daughter Mary Ann married Enoch Davies, a lead miner from Cardiganshire. In 1899 daughter Margaret died aged 12. Meanwhile, between 1891 and 1896, four more children were born to Thomas and Sarah, namely: Benjamin, Gwendoline, Myfanwy and Llewellyn George. So, living at Llanerchi in 1901 were: Thomas (now employed on the dams), Sarah Ann, Mary Ann, Sarah, Benjamin, Gwendoline, Myfanwy, Llewellyn, a grandson John, son-in-law Enoch and a lodger. Sons David and Albert Edward had gone to work for their grandfather at Pant-y-blodau, while Evan appears to have been working at the Rhiwnant in the Claerwen valley. Eldest son Thomas had moved away, married Magdalene Evans and was working as a farm bailiff in Rhosferig fach near Builth. John Pryce Davies also appears to have moved away to work as a waggoner in Abergwesyn.

Llanerchi was dealt with under the Houses of the Working Classes Act. No proposals were made by the Corporation, as the property would not be affected and it was believed that the tenant, who was working for the Corporation, would remain and find work on farms with his father-in-law. However, the tenant expressed a wish to stay on at Llanerchi. The house itself was in a very poor state, but with the Corporation's approval it was hoped that the house and a few fields could be set aside at a rent of £12 per year.

Thomas's wife Sarah died in 1904, and by 1906 the family had moved out and were now living at Marchnant in the Claerwen valley, where Gwendoline died in 1907. By 1911, Thomas was farming at Marchnant with his son Evan as a shepherd, and daughter Sarah was housekeeping for them. Also living at Marchnant was a son, Llewellyn George, and a grandson. Myfanwy was working as a servant at the neighbouring farm of Llanerch-y-cawr. Mary Ann had moved just outside the valley to live at Llanfadog hut, which had been built by the Corporation to house workers. Mary's husband Enoch was now employed as a labourer by the Corporation, and eldest son Thomas was living in Garth near Builth, and was now employed as a road labourer for the Council.

The fate of the other family members is less clear. David and Albert Edward appear to have been working as railway labourers in Birmingham, and were both living on the same street in the city, lodging with families. It is not known if the Birmingham connection resulted from what happened in the valley or if this is just a coincidence; however, by 1918 they had returned home to the valley, and war records show that they lived at T'yn-y-pant, one of the replacement cottages. As for John Pryce Davies, it appears that he had moved from Abergwesyn further south to Llanelli, married and was employed as a haulier on the Great Western Railway.

Today a few remains of Llanerchi can be found in the forestry plantation above the new Nant-Gwyllt Church (*see p. 166*).

31. GLAN-YR-AFON

This was home to labourer Howell Lewis, his wife Mary and their two daughters, Elizabeth and Esther. They had a son, also named Howell, who was working as a farm servant at Allt-goch for the Hughes family.

By 1901, the family were still at Glan-yr-afon, Howell now employed as a roadman, and Howell Jnr working as a stone labourer, probably on the works. Daughter Elizabeth had moved to work as a domestic servant at Termynydd – a bungalow built by the Corporation close to Nant-Gwyllt House, where the civil engineer Herbert Atkinson and his family lived.

Glan-yr-afon would be submerged under the Caban-coch reservoir, and by 1905 the family had left their home. Under the Houses of the Working Classes Act the Corporation had to replace this property and provide a new home for Howell and his family, and it was planned that he be rehoused in a newly-built cottage close to Pen-y-gareg Farm further up the valley. This was thought to be a better location for the job of a roadman looking after roads in the upper Elan Valley. The cottage was built, but it does not appear that Howell and his family ever lived there, as by 1911 Howell, now retired, and his wife Mary were living at Glanrhydwen, nearer to the village of Cwmdeuddwr.

Son Howell married in 1902, and by 1911 he was living in Abercynon, Glamorganshire, working as a coal miner. At some point after the family left their home, youngest daughter Esther travelled to America where, in 1912, she married Charles Carpenter in Chicago. He was employed as an accountant for the US Government. Esther made many voyages home to Rhayader to visit her family.

32. NANT-GWYLLT SCHOOL

The school would be lost under the waters of the Caban-coch reservoir. In 1891 the school was run by the Abley sisters: Elizabeth the school mistress with Alice Anne assisting her. In 1894 Alice Anne married Evan Jones, a farmer from Upper Llanfadog. The following year her sister Elizabeth married Thomas Baynham, a policeman, and by 1901 they had left and the school was uninhabited.

A group of pupils and teachers outside Nant-Gwyllt School (32). Standing on the left is Elizabeth Abley, with her sister, Alice Anne, standing on the right (*Betty Davies Collection*)

In 1901 Alice Anne was living with her husband just beyond the construction site of the Caban-coch dam at Upper Llanfadog farm, and Elizabeth was teaching in Boughrood, Radnorshire. In 1908 Alice Anne's husband died and she remarried in 1910. Her new husband was John Jones from Cerig-cwplau in the Claerwen valley, and they continued farming at Upper Llanfadog. By 1911 Elizabeth was still teaching in Radnorshire, but had moved to a school in Norton.

The school had been leased to Miss Margaret Gertrude Lewis Lloyd, and in 1902 she assigned her interest in the lease to the Corporation for £150. The school was further conveyed to the Corporation in 1905 by the Lewis Lloyd family. The school would be replaced and rebuilt in the Elan Village.

33. NANT-GWYLLT CHURCH

As the church would be submerged by the Caban-coch reservoir, the building was conveyed to the Corporation by the Ecclesiastical Commissioners in exchange for the building of a new church.

In 1895 an appeal was made by local clergymen to the Corporation for an extension to be built onto the old church so that they could offer services to more people, now that the population was being increased by the influx of new workers. However, this appeal failed. By 1900 the new church had been built and was in use, situated above the construction site of the Gareg-ddu viaduct. The old church was demolished

Nant-Gwyllt Church (33) (*by permission of Powys Archives R/D/CL/1/25*)

The interior of Nant-Gwyllt Church (33) looking east (*Betty Davies Collection*)

prior to being submerged. Upon the church's demolition, the bell was taken and erected on the new church, and a marble tablet commemorating the Lewis Lloyd family was removed and re-erected inside the new church.

34. Ty-bach
Ty-bach was unoccupied in 1891, but at some time during the construction of the dams it was the home of a local preacher and his wife, and used as a refreshment house. The cottage would be flooded by the Caban-coch reservoir.

35. Tan-y-foel
A large family of nine lived here in 1891. The cottage was home to Benjamin Davies, a tailor, his wife Elizabeth and their son Benjamin, also a tailor. Their widowed daughter Margaret Evans also lived with them, together with her children: Jonathan, Sarah Ann, Elizabeth, Margaret and Jane.

Tan-y-foel would be submerged under the waters of Caban-coch reservoir, for which Benjamin received £2 10s compensation for his land being taken, and a rent reduction from £5 to £3. Under the scheme to rehouse the working classes the Corporation had to provide a replacement cottage for Tan-y-foel. This was duly built and called

Llanfadog cottage, and was situated just across the road from the newly-built Baptist Chapel. By 1901 Benjamin and his wife were living at the new cottage, along with a son, David, who had returned to work on the dams. Also living there were two of their grandchildren and four lodgers who were employed on the works. It seems that Benjamin and his family were the only residents affected by the scheme who ended up living in a replacement cottage that was actually built for them. None of the other five cottages ever housed the people they were intended for as a result of the scheme. In 1904 Benjamin died, and his wife Elizabeth remained at the cottage, being joined in 1911 by another son, John.

Llanfadog cottage, built to replace Tan-y-foel, still stands opposite the new Baptist Chapel

Son Benjamin had married around 1894, and in 1901 he was living across the road from his parents in the new Baptist Chapel house. He was still tailoring but was also caretaker of the chapel, while his wife was housekeeper for the Minister. Benjamin was also the first organist at the new chapel. By 1911 the couple were living a little further along the road to Cwmdeuddwr, at one of the Llanfadog Bungalows built by the Corporation for workers. At some point they also ran Llanfadog Stores.

In 1899 their widowed daughter Margaret married John Henry Roberts, a labourer on the works, and in 1901 they were living in the Claerwen valley at Pen-rhiwlan, where her husband was listed as a navvy. The couple also had three children and four lodgers living with them. After the works finished they moved north, and in 1911 they were living in Salford, Manchester where John Henry was employed as a builder's labourer. Two of Margaret's daughters, Jane and Elizabeth, were also in the same area working as domestic servants. Margaret's son Jonathan, who was living with his grandparents in 1901 and was employed as a blacksmith, had, by 1911, moved to Abercynon, Glamorganshire, where he was lodging with Howell Lewis (formerly of Glan-yr-afon) and was employed in a colliery.

With the family gone from Tan-y-foel, by 1901 the cottage housed workers prior to being flooded.

Tan-y-foel (35) with Abernant (36) on the opposite side and further along the road to Rhayader

36. ABERNANT
Seth Thomas, the Baptist Minister, lived here and, together with his wife Mary Ann, ran a shop. They also employed a domestic servant, Elizabeth Ann Meredith, who was from Cwm-clyd in the Claerwen valley.

Mary Ann died in 1893 and Seth in 1899. Before his death, Seth applied to run a grocer's shop in the Elan Village. This was granted, and by 1901 Seth's stepson, Thomas Charles Griffiths, was running this shop along with his wife. Thomas had married Elizabeth Ann Meredith, Seth's domestic servant, in 1897.

TOP: The same location as shown on p. 117, but looking in the opposite direction towards Nant-Gwyllt. Abernant (36) is in the right foreground (*by permission of Powys Archives B/DX/36/110*). BOTTOM: A similar viewpoint in 2018, from the top of the Caban-coch dam, looking west

In 1901 Abernant was still being run as a grocers and bakers by incomers to the valley, who were probably employed by Thomas. In 1904 Thomas Charles Griffiths died and at this time it also appears that the family were back at Abernant prior to it being submerged. By 1911 Thomas's widow, Elizabeth Ann, had moved away and was living in Builth with her family.

37. Gro Mill

The mill was run by the Lloyd family. It was used both for sawing timber and for milling crops, and attached to it was a kiln house. John Lloyd, a carpenter, his wife Margaret and their sons, Thomas (also a carpenter) and Llewellyn (a farmer) were living at the Mill in 1891.

The view across the wide valley floor towards Nant-Gwyllt in 1897, just showing the Mill (37) in the bottom left-hand corner close to Nant-Gwyllt Church (33) (*Richard Hughes Collection*)

John's wife Margaret passed away in 1892, and was probably the last burial at the old Baptist Chapel on 23 December of that year. It would not be long before they would have to lift her remains and have them reinterred in the new Baptist Chapel graveyard at Llanfadog.

In 1896 the Lloyds received the sum of £5 10s in compensation for land taken by the works, and a reduction in their rent. Later in 1896 the Lloyd family had begun, without permission, to convert the kiln house into a dwelling. They then asked the Corporation if they could make extensions to the property by adding rooms along the roadside. This was not agreed to as the extension was on land that had already been taken by the works, and the Corporation did not think it wise to allow people to re-establish themselves on land already given up to the Corporation.

By 1901 John was now listed as a farmer, son Thomas still listed as a carpenter and Llewellyn as a butcher. An older daughter, Margaret, had returned to keep house for the family. John had also employed another butcher, a butcher's apprentice, a wag-goner and a housemaid. As already noted, John Lloyd did not want to be considered for rehousing under the Act, as he regarded himself as a farmer of 33 acres with a flock of 60 sheep, and proprietor of a butcher's business.

There is a record of a John and Llewellyn Lloyd becoming tenants of Gro farm with 500 sheep, which in 1904 was taken over by John Jones of Talwrn farm in Llanwrthwl. The flock would be reduced to 400 sheep, and John Jones would have to pay the Lloyd family 22 shillings per head for the surplus. This area was quite late to be flooded even though the dams were opened in 1904 (the Caban-coch reservoir would not flood until the winter of 1905). During this period Gro farm would be let on a weekly basis pending submergence.

The Mill would eventually be flooded by the Caban-coch reservoir and, by 1906, the Lloyd family had made the short move to live in Rhayader. In 1911 they were living at Glanrhos in East Street. John had by now retired, son Llewellyn was still working as a butcher, and Thomas had married in 1902 and was now employed as a carpenter by the Corporation.

38. Gro-isaf

This was occupied by a carpenter, David Jones, who was to cause a few problems for the Corporation: firstly, he refused the Corporation access to the house when they wanted to survey the property; then, in 1898 the Missioner in the Elan Village was voicing his concerns about David Jones' behaviour. The following is a transcription of a letter from the Missioner to Stephen Williams, the Corporation's agent.

It is not known what action was subsequently taken, but in the parish registers for Cwmdeuddwr there is evidence to show that David Jones died in 1899 while in the Rhayader Union Workhouse.

Birmingham Corporation Water Works
Missioner's Hut
J.B.Higham. B.A.   Elan Village
Missioner   Near Rhayader
Radnorshire

June 24th 1898

Dear Sir,

In visiting about the valley, I find that David Jones, residing at
Gro Isaf, conducts himself in a most insanitary and uncivilized
manner. He drinks heavily, and last week encouraged a man to
frequent the house, who in a drunken fit nearly killed the man,
to whom David Jones has sublet the greater part of the cottage,
others present assisted to expel the assailant, but they too were
badly hurt in the encounter. I state these particulars, as I consider unless the said David Jones be warned to conduct himself
better, he might at any time in a drunken fit set his cottage on
fire or cause some harm to other occupants of the place. Will you
kindly let me know whether he has any permanent claim upon
the Corporation whereby he can demand to reside at Gro Isaf, in
spite of his filthy and dangerous ways.

Yours, faithfully

S. Williams, Esq, Rhayader   J.B. Higham

Transcribed from Powys County Archives R/D/WWA/1/655

By 1901 Gro-isaf was occupied by 12 workers. The house would eventually be submerged under the waters of the Caban-coch reservoir.

The following two pictures (*see overleaf*) show the area occupied by Nant-Gwyllt
School, Nant-Gwyllt Church, Gro Mill, Ty-bach, Tan-y-foel, Abernant, Gro-isaf and
Gro-bach. The images record the scene prior to the works starting and then again soon
after the valley had been flooded by the Caban-coch reservoir.

View of Caban Coch Reservoir before Construction

Rhayader, Caban Coch Reservoir

TOP: The valley before flooding. Nant-Gwyllt school can be seen in the left of the picture
BOTTOM: A similar view after the flooding of the valley

39. Gro-bach

This was home to Ann Morgans, a widow living on parish relief, along with her daughter Sybil Jane, and her grandchildren, Selina Beatrice Jones and Evan Thomas.

In 1893 Sybil Jane married David Rees, and by 1898 the family had left the valley to live at Pontprenddu in Llanfihangel Brynpabau near Newbridge-on-Wye, where David was employed as a shepherd. Sybil's mother Ann died there in 1898, and was buried in Cwmdeuddwr churchyard.

Sybil Jane died in 1906, and by 1911 David was living in Newbridge-on-Wye with his children and a housekeeper, and was still employed as a shepherd.

By 1901 Evan Thomas had moved to Abergwesyn, working as a waggoner. He married in 1903 and remained in Abergwesyn.

In 1901 Selina Beatrice Jones was living with her uncle, William Roberts (formerly of Blaen-Coel) at Erwllyn in Llanwrthwl, and by 1911 she was working as a domestic servant at the Talwrn farm, situated above the Elan Village. Later that year she married John Edward Jones and went on to live in Cilmery near Builth Wells.

40. (No. 1) Nant-Gwyllt cottage

This was one of two cottages built for servants of the Lewis Lloyd family at Nant-Gwyllt House; this one being occupied in 1891 by a gardener, David Vaughan, and a coachman, Walter Norbury.

In 1891 David married Sarah Rees Lloyd in London, and following the sale of Nant-Gwyllt House to the Corporation in 1893 they moved to Bryntirion Lodge just north of Rhayader (the Lewis Lloyd family having purchased Bryntirion House). Here, David remained as a gardener in the service of the family.

It is not known if Walter was released by the Lewis Lloyd family, or if he chose to leave after the sale of the house, but he moved down to South Wales and found work as a sinker in the coal mines. In 1895 he was one of six men who were killed in an accident at Abercynon Colliery. His body was brought home for burial in Nantmel churchyard.

41. (No. 2) Nant-Gwyllt cottage

The second cottage was occupied by the Conway family. They were not servants of the Lewis Lloyd family, but a family connected with lead mining in the area. In 1891 the cottage was home to Anne Conway and her sons, George, Edward, Samuel, Benjamin, and daughter Hettie. At this time, Anne's husband Edward was up at Dalrhiw, mining in the Rhiwnant valley in the neighbouring parish of Llanwrthwl, and the family would soon join him there. In 1897, son George died. This was followed in 1899 by the death of his father, Edward.

By 1901 those living at Dalrhiw were Anne, her sons Benjamin and Edward (both still lead mining), and daughter Hettie. Samuel had married in 1900 and by 1901 he was the publican running the Bell Inn in Cwmdeuddwr.

The mining in the Rhiwnant valley would come to an end with the completion of the works. In 1903 daughter Hettie married Gilbert Hill Jones from nearby Marchnant farm and they moved to a farm in Llanyre, a few miles south of Rhayader. It appears that some of the family moved there with them, because in 1907 Hettie's mother Anne died there, and her brother Benjamin also died there in 1911. By 1911 Samuel was still publican at the Bell Inn, and brother Edward (now listed as a former miner) was living at Ty'n-y-gors in the Claerwen valley – along with a sister, Elizabeth Margaret, who had returned to the area after working away in London.

Both cottages were used during the works for the accommodation of office workers, but they would both be submerged under the Caban-coch reservoir.

42. Nant-Gwyllt Lodge

The lodge was situated at the top of the drive leading to Nant-Gwyllt House, and adjacent to the junction of the rivers Elan and Claerwen. It was home to the Lloyd family, who were gamekeepers in the employment of the Lewis Lloyd family.

Living there in 1891 were Edward Lloyd and his wife Mary and their four sons: Edward (also a gamekeeper), Alfred William, Thomas and Arthur Henry. Their daughter Catherine was working as a servant at Cwm-Elan House.

By 1901 the family had left Nant-Gwyllt Lodge and moved to a farmstead called Troedrhiwfelen closer to the village of Cwmdeuddwr. Living there at that time were Edward (still employed as a gamekeeper), his wife Mary and two of their sons: Thomas, now employed on the works, and Arthur Henry. Eldest son Edward was living up near Claerwen farm, and was employed as a gamekeeper. Alfred William had moved to Bewdley in Worcestershire, where he worked as a coachman (possibly for the Corporation, as he was lodging in the same house as Thomas Richard Morgans from Dol-folau). Daughter Catherine appears to have moved away to work as a housemaid for a Justice of the Peace in Aberedw.

A couple of marriages followed. Firstly, Catherine married Albert Edwin Price in 1902 (the couple remaining in Aberedw near Builth Wells), and her brother Alfred William married Minnie Sarah Westgate in Eastbourne, Sussex in 1907.

By 1911 Edward and Mary were still at Troedrhiwfelen, along with son Edward. At this time Edward was still working as a gamekeeper, and son Edward was employed as an estate labourer for the Corporation. Alfred William had returned home and was living at Sunnyside in Rhayader, still employed as a coachman. Also living with him at Sunnyside was his brother Arthur Henry, who was now employed as a chauffeur. Later in 1911 Arthur Henry would marry Emily Elizabeth Gertrude Williams in Rhayader. The Lodge would be submerged under the Caban-coch reservoir, but during the construction of the dams it was taken over by workers.

Rhayader. Elan Valley Junction of Rivers Elan and Claer...

Nant-Gwyllt Lodge (42) on the right and Nant-Gwyllt House in the distance (c.1890s)

43. Gro-uchaf

Another large family, the Prices, lived at Gro-uchaf. In 1891 this consisted of farmer, Thomas Price and his wife Selina; their three daughters, Emmeline, Agnes and Martha; their two sons, William Dyke and Thomas Powell; two stepsons, Daniel Henry and Thomas Alfred Edwards, together with a nephew, William Hughes, who was working as a farm servant – ten in all.

Between 1891 and 1901 there were three marriages in the family. In 1896 daughter Emmeline married David Price Pugh, a shepherd from Nant-y-Car a little further up the valley. In 1898 Martha, who had been working at the Bell Inn in Cwmdeuddwr, married Pryce Lewis Jones, a booking clerk at Rhayader Station. The following year William Dyke Price married Sarah Jane Hamer from Cwmdeuddwr.

By 1901 John Price and his family had moved into Gro-uchaf from Marchnant, about one mile up the valley. A hut had been built close to Gro-uchaf for the accommodation of workers, and this was being run by Selina as housekeeper. Living with her was son Thomas Powell Price and a further two children born between 1891 and 1901. Husband Thomas was away visiting the farm of Crownant near Llanwrthwl. The hut was home to seven stone quarrymen employed on the works.

At this time, daughter Emmeline had moved with her husband, who was shepherding, to Merthyr Cynog near Builth. Martha had also moved in the same direction, her husband now the station master in Aberedw. Son William Dyke was living at Neuadd-fach (the home of his wife), closer to the village of Cwmdeuddwr where he was employed as a stone driller on the works. William's sister Agnes was living with her older, married sister Harriet at Penpistyll in Nantmel, where she was working as a dressmaker. Of the stepsons, Daniel was working as a grocer's assistant in the Elan Village, and Thomas had moved to Llandrindod Wells where he was employed as an apprentice monumental mason.

In 1902 daughter Agnes married Richard Johns, an Australian of Cornish descent who was a blacksmith on the works. After the dams were finished, they moved away to live and work in Constantine, Cornwall, but would return in later life to live in Rhayader. By 1911, with the works now over, Thomas and Selina had settled at Crownant farm in Llanwrthwl, along with son Thomas Powell Price. Emmeline was living in Garth near Builth where husband David was a shepherd. William Dyke was still at Neuadd-fach, but now farming, and Martha was still at Aberedw where her husband remained the station master. Stepson Daniel had moved away and married, and was living in Bargoed, Glamorganshire where he was a fruit merchant, employing two assistants, a nursemaid and a domestic servant.

Gro-uchaf farm would be submerged under the Caban-coch reservoir.

44. Nant-Gwyllt House

This mansion house was home to Robert Lewis Lloyd and his family, the owners of the largest portion of the watershed to be sold to the Birmingham Corporation. Robert was a barrister and also County Councillor for Radnorshire and Justice of the Peace.

Nant-Gwyllt House (44) in the 1890s (*Richard Hughes Collection*)

Residing at the house in 1891 were Robert Lewis Lloyd and his wife Mary Anne Jane together with their children: Robert Wharton (a solicitor's clerk), James Edward, Louisa Beatrice, Mary Anne Jane, Cecilia Joan and Gertrude Constance. The staff consisted of a butler, Evan Roderick; ladies' maid, Eliza Anne Lloyd; housemaids, Laura Elinor Mitchell and Alice Leighton; laundry maid, Jessie Tompkins; kitchen maid, Anne Davies; footman, Thomas Richard Mills; and cook, Pericia Hayes. There were also people staying at the house as visitors.

Another view of Nant-Gwyllt House (44) in the 1890s (*Betty Davies Collection*)

Following negotiations, Robert soon agreed in 1893 to sell all his land and holdings within the watershed to the Corporation. After this the household broke up, and the staff had to find alternative work. With the money from the sale, Robert purchased Bryntirion House to the north of Rhayader, and the Otterhead Estate on the borders of Somerset and Devon. Before leaving, daughter Mary Anne Jane Lewis Lloyd married Sidney Cooke Lewis in the old Nant-Gwyllt Church. Sidney was one of the civil engineers living at Cwm-Elan House in 1891. In September 1893 the *Montgomery County Times* reported that the inhabitants of the valley had made a collection for the Lewis Lloyd family, now that they were departing for Devon. The sum of £70 was raised and the items purchased were a pair of candelabra, a pair of silver fruit dishes and an illuminated address in a gold frame expressing the regrets and good wishes of the locals. In November 1893 Robert Wharton Lewis Lloyd married Elizabeth Alice Evan Williams in Rhayader. She was the daughter of Samuel Charles Evan Williams, a staunch supporter of the fight to preserve the rights of the commoners and tenants during the period when the Bill was going through Parliament, and the former owner of Bryntirion. In 1894 son James Edward Lewis Lloyd was listed as a 2nd Lieutenant in the 1st Herefordshire Volunteer Rifle Corps. He later became Captain before being transferred to the Devonshire Regiment as a 2nd Lieutenant in 1900. Also around this time, James appears on the electoral roll living in furnished rooms at the Noyadd in Cwmdeuddwr, home of Benjamin Pugh Lewis.

So by 1901, living at their new home, Otterhead House, were Robert and his wife, along with daughters Cecilia Joan and Gertrude Constance. None of the staff from Nant-Gwyllt House were employed there, but working for them was a former house-maid from Bryntirion and another housemaid, Catherine Davies from the Rhiwnant farm in the Claerwen valley. Son Robert Wharton Lewis Lloyd had gone to live at Bryntirion House, and his sister Mary Anne Jane, who had married Sidney Cooke Lewis, appears to have stayed in the area until about 1896 because of Sidney's work. However, by 1901 the couple had moved to Kidderminster in Worcestershire, and her sister Louisa Beatrice was also living with them.

Of the staff members, in 1898 butler Evan Roderick married ladies' maid Eliza Anne Lloyd in Milford Haven, and by 1901 Evan was the proprietor of the Imperial Hotel in Llandeilo fawr, Carmarthenshire. Housemaid, Laura Elinor Mitchell had returned home to Gloucestershire where she married a railway worker, and her fellow housemaid, Alice Leighton, was employed as a cook in Tewkesbury, Worcestershire. Footman, Thomas Richard Mills, who was the only local in the employment of the Lewis Lloyd family and hailed from Nantmel, was now employed as butler for a brewer in Llanelli, Carmarthenshire.

In February 1905 Robert Wharton Lewis Lloyd died at Bryntirion following a fall from a window. Later in 1905 his father, after failing to find a buyer for the Otterhead Estate, sold off the furniture and effects by auction and let out the house and estate, and then moved to Bath. James Edward Lewis Lloyd had been promoted to Lieutenant in 1902, but by 1907 he had left the Army and sailed from Southampton for New York, his occupation listed as a surveyor. By 1911 Robert and his wife, along with daughters Cecilia Joan and Gertrude Constance, were living at 16 Somerset Place, Bath. Louisa Beatrice was living with her uncle in Machynlleth and Mary Anne Jane was living with her husband, Sidney Cooke Lewis in Bromley, Kent. James Edward Lewis Lloyd had made his way to Canada where, in September of 1911, he died from the excesses of alcohol at Owen Sound County Gaol, Ontario (his occupation at this time given as labourer).

In 1911, the staff members for whom records could be found were: Evan Roderick and his wife (still keeping a hotel in Llandeilo); Laura Elinor Mitchell (still in

Gloucester and now with a family of her own), and Alice Leighton (still a cook, but living in London). Thomas Richard Mills married in 1904, and had progressed from butler to being a hotel proprietor and brewery agent at the Salutation Inn in Llanelli.

There were two further sons of Robert and Mary Anne Jane Lewis Lloyd, neither living at home in 1891 nor at the time of the sale of Nant-Gwyllt House. Thomas Price Lewis Lloyd emigrated to America in around 1890, became an American citizen in 1895 and settled in California as a farmer. A younger brother, George Lewis Lloyd, had joined the Army by 1894 and saw service with the South Wales Borderers, the Royal Malta Artillery and the Middlesex Regiment. In 1899, by now a Lieutenant, he was seconded to the Colonial Office and sent to Nigeria. By 1905 he had moved to Middelburg in the Transvaal region of South Africa, and was now a Captain. He married here and had a son, Robert, in 1906. Unfortunately George's son died as a baby and his marriage did not last. He left the Army, and by 1908 had moved to Canada where he initially settled in Alberta, becoming a Canadian citizen, before eventually moving to British Columbia.

Nant-Gwyllt House was used by the Corporation during the time of the works, then demolished and submerged by the Caban-coch reservoir. At times of low water levels, some of the garden walls of the house and a bridge reappear (*see pp. 168–169*). Interestingly, found in a walled-up recess when the house was being dismantled, was a 40-inch wooden-handled rapier sword dating to around 1750. Many of the Lewis Lloyd family are buried in Cwmdeuddwr churchyard. A large monument marks their resting place, and there are also memorial plaques inside the church.

A strange coincidence concerning the Otterhead Estate is that, following various lettings, the property was sold in 1939 and purchased by Taunton Corporation for use as a water catchment area.

45. Pant-y-blodau

This was home to Evan Jones, who farmed across the river at Nant-Gwyllt farm. Living with Evan were his wife Margaret; two of his grandsons from Llanerchi, William and Thomas Davies; a labourer, Edward Evans; and house servant, Clara Meredith from Cwm-clyd, a little further up the valley. By 1901 little had altered, except that two different grandsons (Albert and David Davies, also from Llanerchi) were now helping him, while the house servant, Clara, had moved. They also had a labourer lodging with them.

In 1902 Evan's wife Margaret died. Evan stayed on at Pant-y-blodau until 1905, when it was due to be flooded by the Caban-coch reservoir, at which point Evan and his labourer Edward Evans moved just a short distance to farm at Penrhiw closer to the village of Llanwrthwl, where Evan died in 1907. Edward Evans continued to farm at Penrhiw.

46. Pen-glan-Einon

This property would be unaffected by the works, it being situated high above the River Claerwen. The Meredith family lived here, consisting of farm labourer Evan and his wife Ann; their three daughters, Lizzie, Naomi, Ruth Gladys, and their son George. Also boarding with them were Teddy and Margaret Hallybone from London (two children who appear to be Evan and Ann's grandchildren).

In 1898, daughter Naomi married John Evans, a labourer, and by 1901 the couple were living at Domen cottage in Cwmdeuddwr. In February 1900 Ruth Gladys married Walter Price, the son of John Price from Marchnant just across the valley. By 1901 they had moved to Aberdare in South Wales, where Walter was a coal miner. Back at Pen-glan-Einon in 1901 were Evan and Ann plus son George and granddaughter Margaret. They also had a labourer lodging with them, John Morris, who was employed on the works.

As noted previously, an older daughter, Annie, had returned home to marry James Jones from the Henfron in 1891, after which they left for Mountain Ash. Many more members of the family also ended up in the Aberdare/ Mountain Ash area. In 1901 Teddy Hallybone was lodging with Annie and working as a colliery lampman. His sister Margaret soon joined them, having married collier John Morris in Aberdare in 1903. This was the same John Morris who had been lodging at Pen-glan-Einon in 1901, and the couple remained in the area, as did Ruth Gladys and her husband Walter. Also by 1911, Naomi had left Cwmdeuddwr and joined the exodus to South Wales, living in Caerau near Maesteg where her husband was working in the coal mines. Teddy made a return to the valley and worked on the scheme for a while, but by 1911 had gone back to the Mountain Ash area to work in the mines there.

Back at home in the valley, deaths occurred in the family: firstly son George in 1909, then a year later Evan's wife passed away, leaving Evan living alone at Pen-glan-Einon where he was listed as farmer and part-time Post Office official. Evan also became sexton of the newly built Nant-Gwyllt Church.

Today Pen-glan-Einon is let as a holiday cottage.

47. Pen-cae-haidd

This was home to the Lawrence family: father John, a waggoner; three sons, John, Jacob and Richard; and three daughters, Eliza (who kept house), Margaret and Caroline. Also living with them was grandson, John Price. There was another daughter, Jane Lawrence, who worked away from home as a servant, but still in the valley, at Ty-nant (1891), Alltgoch (1901) and Cwm-clyd (1911).

The farm would remain and be unaffected by the building of the dams and reservoirs. In 1898 father John Lawrence died. *The Montgomery and Radnor Echo* reported that, while working with his neighbour Evan Meredith, he had fallen from the top of a load on a gambo (farm cart) and broken his spine. The inquest, which was held at

Nant-Gwyllt House, attributed this as the cause of death. The funeral was held a few days later and was said to have been one of the largest ever seen in the neighbourhood. John was buried in Cwmdeuddwr churchyard.

Daughter Eliza took over the farm with the help of her nephew, John Price. Besides seeing to the farm, Eliza had to look after all of her brothers and sisters living at home, who were unkindly described in the censuses as, for example, 'feeble minded' (1901 census). The property later became abandoned and fell into ruins.

48. Pant-tawel

Unoccupied in 1891, this was the former home of Margaret Powell who, at this time, was living a little further up the valley keeping house for John Jones, a farmer and weaver at Llwyn-dale. Later in 1891 she married John Jones, and by 1901 had moved back to Pant-tawel. John died in 1901 and Margaret a year later in 1902.

Pant-tawel would remain standing, but would be virtually cut off by the Caban-coch reservoir, because of which the property became abandoned.

49. Dol-y-mynach

Dol-y-mynach, the third large house in the valley, was farmed by the Williams family. In 1891 it was occupied by David Williams and his wife Jane; their four sons, John Thomas, David Alfred, Benjamin and Llewellyn; their two daughters, Catherine and Sarah, together with a farm servant by the name of John Jones who came from Cil-oerwynt. By the time of the 1901 census, much remained the same: daughter Catherine had married John Jones from Cwm-Coel in 1900; and later, in 1901, John Thomas married Mary Price from Pen-henbren. The family also had a niece and a grandson living with them, along with three boarders who were working on the dams. Son Llewellyn was living with his maternal grandmother in Narberth, Pembrokeshire, where he was employed as an apprentice cabinet maker.

Under the original scheme this large, historically significant house would be too close to the Dol-y-mynach reservoir (due to be completed in the second phase of the works, some 20–30 years later), and therefore the house was demolished. However, advances in technology meant that this dam was never completed; and whereas the original plan of the second phase was for three dams on the Claerwen river, this was replaced by one scheme for a single, large concrete dam further up the valley. The outcome of this meant that the remains of Dol-y-mynach were left high and dry, and maybe it need not have been taken down. The house stood at an elevation of 900 feet, and at the end of the first phase the water level in the partly completed Dol-y-mynach reservoir was 830 feet, with the eventual top water level due to be 900 feet at the end of the second phase. Why the house was taken down so soon, when others were not, is not known.

With the house gone, by 1911 the family had broken up and dispersed, with David, his wife Jane and sons Benjamin and Llewellyn moving less than a mile further up the

TOP: The River Claerwen and, across the meadow, Dol-y-mynach (49) in 1892
(*by permission of the Library of Birmingham MS944 BCC ST 2008/214/ Box 45*).
BOTTOM: The site of Dol-y-mynach (49) in 2018 from roughly the same viewpoint

valley to farm at Cwm-clyd. Here they also employed a farm servant, Jane Lawrence, who originated from Pen-cae-haidd. John Thomas was farming at Cil-oerwynt, the next farm up the valley on the Radnorshire side of the river. Catherine and her husband John Jones had gone to farm at Dyffryn in the parish of Nantmel, and David Alfred went to farm at the Lingen in St Harmon where his sister Sarah was housekeeping for him.

Very little seems to be known of the house's history, apart from its connections with the monks of Strata Florida. Although taken down, the house was mentioned in a 1911 survey of ancient monuments, which stated, 'The old house, once standing within the meadow, has recently been razed by its owners; its roof tiles, oaken beam of an open fireplace, and walls are said to have denoted a high antiquity'. Today, only an old barn belonging to Dol-y-mynach remains, and the area with its ponds is used for educational purposes, to study the water habitat.

50. Marchnant

This farm, on the opposite side of the river to Dol-y-mynach, was home to John Price, a shepherd, and his family: his wife Elizabeth, their sons William and Richard, and daughters Elizabeth and Gertrude Ann. There was also another son, Walter, who was employed as a farm servant at nearby Llanerch-y-cawr. By 1901 the family had moved a little way down the valley to live at Gro-uchaf where John was still shepherding, and sons William and Richard were employed as agricultural labourers; daughter Elizabeth had moved out to find work. Walter had married Ruth Gladys Meredith of Pen-glan-Einon in 1900, and they had gone to live in Aberdare, South Wales, where Walter was a coal miner. By 1901 Marchnant had been taken over by farmer Gilbert Hill Jones whose father William had taken the tenancy of the farm on one of the new 21-year leases being offered by the Corporation.

In 1902 daughter Elizabeth had married Thomas Rowlands who had been working across the river at Gro Mill. In 1904 son William died at the age of 19, followed in 1909 by the death of his father, John.

So, by 1911 the remaining members of the family had left the valley, and John's wife Elizabeth was living at Cornhill Cottage in Rhayader. In an interesting point noted on the 1911 census, Elizabeth states that she has nine children – three still alive, four who had died and a further two for whom she could not say whether they were alive or dead.

Son Walter was now employed as a mine repairer in Aberdare; daughter Elizabeth had moved with her husband to a farm near Llanidloes in Montgomeryshire, and Gertrude Ann was working as a servant at Park farm in Cwmdeuddwr. Son Richard initially found work on the dams before following his brother Walter down to Aberdare to work in the coal mines. Sadly, he died from meningitis in 1910 at the age of 23. Under the original scheme, Marchnant was due to be demolished and replaced, as it would have been too close to the shore of the reservoir; however, as noted previously, the plans were altered. A replacement cottage was built for Marchnant, which the Corporation named Ty'n-y-gors Cottage, as there was already a property close by named Ty'n-y-gors. This replacement cottage is sometimes referred to as New Marchnant. The 1911 census records that the Davies family from Llanerchi had come to live at Marchnant, which probably refers to the replacement cottage. The 1918 electoral roll for Llanwrthwl offers further clarification of this, as it lists Samuel Conway living at Marchnant and Margaret Conway living at Ty'n-y-gors. Both were connected with the Conway family, formerly of Nant-Gwyllt cottage (41) and Dalrhiw (55); while Evan Davies, formerly of Llanerchi (30), was living at New Marchnant, which looks to be the replacement cottage built by the Corporation as Ty'n-y-gors Cottage. The original Marchnant was later abandoned. Early in 2019 the replacement cottage was put up for rent by the Elan Valley Trust, and referred to as Marchnant Cottage.

51. Pen-rhiwlan

This was a small, two-roomed cottage, all that was left of a once larger farm. In 1891 it was occupied by an agricultural labourer, Thomas Davies. In around 1894 it was discovered that Thomas was living in quite a poor state at the property. Robert Lewis Lloyd and the local doctor were involved, and Thomas was removed to the Rhayader Union Workhouse, and there is some evidence to say that he died there.

Although it was in a bad state of repair, the cottage was used by workers during the building of the dams. Eventually it was abandoned, but would have been lost to the Dol-y-mynach reservoir if this had been completed. Today a few boulders mark the area where the cottage stood (*see p. 167*).

52. Llanerch-y-cawr

Farmer Evan Stephens lived here in 1891 with his wife Ann and their two sons, Thomas Charles and James Evan; their three daughters, Elizabeth, Clara Ann and Margaretta, along with grandson, Winsor Martin Stephens. They also employed four farm servants: Elizabeth Lewis, John Jones, William Meredith from Cwm-clyd and Walter Price from the Marchnant.

Soon after, John Jones, one of the servants, moved on and died later in 1891 while working at Glanllyn farm in Cwmdeuddwr. A number of marriages also took place over the next ten years. In 1892 daughter Elizabeth married David Jones, a mine surveyor from Aberdare; in 1894 Clara Ann married Richard Palfrey Evans; in 1898 Margaretta married Samuel Boucher, an engine fitter on the works from Cornwall; and finally, in 1900, Thomas Charles married Margaret Elizabeth Jones locally, and James Evan married Mary Hardwick in the Birmingham area.

By 1901, living at the farm were Evan and Ann, another son, John William (who had returned home to assist his father in farming), and three new farm servants.

Elizabeth and her husband David had moved to Aberdare where David was a surveyor in a coal mine, Margaretta and her husband were still in the valley at nearby T'yn-y-gors, and her husband was still employed on the works. Thomas Charles and his wife were living in Rhayader, where Thomas was working as a carpenter's labourer. Also living with them was Thomas's son, Winsor Martin. James Evan had moved to Birmingham where he was employed as an omnibus driver.

Later in 1901 John William Stephens married Emmeline Mary Jones from the nearby property of Marchnant. In 1903 Ann Stephens died, followed by her husband Evan in 1907.

By 1911 John William was running Llanerch-y-cawr with his family. Elizabeth was still in Aberdare, and Clara, since her marriage in 1894, had gone to Ferndale in Glamorganshire before returning to Rhayader by 1901, where her husband was employed as a railway carter. They subsequently spent more time in Ferndale; however, by 1911 Clara and her family were living in the parish of Nantmel, while her husband was working as a farm labourer ten miles north-east of Rhayader in Llananno. All this would soon change, however, as in the spring of 1911 Clara's husband Richard emigrated to Western Australia. Clara and their children followed a year later, in 1912, and settled in a place called Narrogin, their address being 'Radnor Vale'.

Margaretta and husband Samuel had moved away, down to the Bridgend area in Glamorganshire, where Margaretta died in 1909. The following year Samuel Boucher emigrated to Melbourne, Australia. Their daughter Phyllis, who had been born in the valley in 1900, was living with her paternal grandmother in Cornwall, but followed her father to Australia in 1913. Thomas Charles had left Rhayader and was now running the Angel Inn in Llanidloes; while his son, Winsor, had moved to Abercynon in South Wales where he was employed in a coal mine (Winsor would return to Rhayader later in his life). Finally, James Evan had left Birmingham and was working as a brake driver in Aberdare.

Llanerch-y-cawr also stood at an elevation of 900 feet (the same as Dol-y-mynach), which meant it would have been right on the edge of the planned reservoir. However, it was not taken down during the first phase and, owing to the change in plans, it survived. The farm would remain and the Stephens family would be there for some years to come. In 1956 a new farmhouse was completed and it is still a working farm today. The old farmhouse is a traditional Welsh longhouse and is now a protected building and let as holiday cottages.

53. T'yn-y-gors

In 1891 this was occupied by Mary Roberts (a widow who was working as a charwoman) and her daughter, Bertha. There were two more daughters: Sarah Jane, working as a servant just up the valley for the Pugh family at Nant-y-Car; and Elizabeth, working closer to the village of Cwmdeuddwr at Penrochan.

In 1893 Elizabeth married Alfred James Morgan, a local farmer, and in 1896 Sarah Jane married John Gwilliam, a gasworks manager originally from Bishops Castle in Shropshire.

By 1901 Mary and Bertha were still at T'yn-y-gors and were joined there by Mary's two sons, John and Matthew, who had been working away and returned home to work on the dams. Elizabeth was with her husband, farming at Gwardolau farm in the parish of Cwmdeuddwr. Sarah Jane and her family had moved around, having spent time in South Wales and Shropshire, before moving to Eynsham in Oxfordshire, where her husband was employed as a gas stoker.

Later in 1901 Matthew died, followed by his mother in 1903. By 1911 Elizabeth was still farming at Gwardolau, but her sister Sarah Jane had moved again, this time down to South Wales to live at Trealaw in the Rhondda Valley where her husband was working as a pipe jointer for the local council.

T'yn-y-gors would remain untouched by the works and still stands today.

54. LLWYN-DALE

This was an old lead miner's cottage in an area that had been mined for several years. In 1887 Sir Joseph Bailey had taken out a licence to work the land for minerals for 21 years in favour of the Builth Lead Mining Company. In 1892 the company assigned the licence to the Corporation for a fee of £8,000. By a further licence of 1892 the Corporation allowed the company to work the mines for a period of seven years, until 1899.

The ruins of Llwyn-dale (54) in the Rhiwnant valley, in 2015

In 1891 the cottage housed farmer John Jones and his housekeeper Margaret Powell, who were soon to be married and would move to Margaret's home, Pant-tawel (48). In 1901 Llwyn-dale had become occupied by George Morgan, a lead miner who had married Emmeline Griffiths from Shop-bach (28). By 1911, George and his family had moved down to South Wales.

The cottage continued to house workers on the dams, but would become abandoned after the works were finished and mining had ceased. The foundations and some walls can still be seen today.

55. DALRHIW

Also a lead miner's cottage, this was occupied by lead miner Edward Conway in 1891, at which time the rest of his family were living elsewhere in the valley, though they would soon join him at Dalrhiw (*see No. 41 Nant-Gwyllt cottage 2*).

The land around the cottage was subject to a licence given to Edward Wood by Robert Lewis Lloyd for 21 years from 1890, in order to search for and win minerals from the land. In 1893 Edward Wood assigned his interest in the licence to the Corporation for a fee of £1,000. Although the cottage would become abandoned, there is some evidence of the Conway family still living there, as the burial of Edward Cleaton Conway in 1917 records his address as Dalrhiw. Remains of the cottage can still be seen today.

56. NANT-Y-CARW MINE

This was a mine situated on the Nant-y-Carw stream just above its junction with the River Rhiwnant, operated by the Builth Lead Mining Company. The mine included a barracks block which housed the workers.

At the time of the 1891 census, five miners were living there, all from outside the area, and mainly Welsh speakers from Cardiganshire. Later in 1892, when Stephen Williams conducted his own census for the Corporation, 18 miners were employed and living at the mine, so numbers here appear to have fluctuated. It seems that the Company was wound up in 1893 and the mine taken over by the Nant-y-Garw Mining Company, which employed 50 men; however, this Company was also wound up in 1897. The Nant-y-Carw mine was included in the agreement made between Sir Joseph Bailey and the Corporation (*see No. 54 Llwyn-dale*). The mine would become abandoned, but remains of it can still be seen today.

57. RHIWNANT

This farm would remain untouched by the works. In 1891 it was occupied by the Davies family, comprising farmer Isaac and his wife Jane, their five daughters, Mary Anna, Catherine Jane, Sarah Ann, Ursula Winifred and Harriet Margaret, along with their son Evan David. They also employed two farm servants, Ann Bennett and Thomas

Meredith (the latter from Cwm-clyd). All was much the same come 1901, though they now had a different farm servant and they also had five boarders – all navvies employed on the works. Daughter Catherine seems to have been entered twice on the 1901 census: at home, listed as a housemaid, and also away from home, employed by the Lewis Lloyd family as a housemaid at their new home at Otterhead.

In February 1909 daughter Sarah Ann died at the age of 24, and later that year in November, on the same day at Llanwrthwl Church, two daughters were married: Mary Anna to farmer Rice Lewis from Tyncoed (a farm closer to Cwmdeuddwr), and Catherine Jane to Henry Cox, a hotel proprietor from Chislehurst in Kent.

By 1911, living at Rhiwnant were Isaac and his wife; although, only a few days after the census was taken, Isaac died. Son Evan David was now assisting with the farming. Also living at home were daughters Harriett Margaret and Mary Anna with her new baby (her husband was still farming at Tyncoed).

Catherine Jane and her husband had moved to Etchingham in Sussex, where Henry was running the Railway Hotel. Ursula Winifred was also away from home, working as a parlour maid in Ford, Shropshire. Catherine Jane, along with her husband, would return to Rhayader, and Ursula Winifred would return to Rhiwnant in later life.

Rhiwnant stayed in the Davies family for many years thereafter and it is still a working farm today.

58. Pen-y-gwaith

This was a disused miners' cottage, unoccupied at the time of the 1891 census; but by the time Stephen Williams had taken his census the following year, Hugh Hughes, a lead miner from Llanwrthwl, had moved in with his wife Jane and son John.

By 1901 Pen-y-gwaith had been taken over by another lead miner, and the Hughes family had moved on. Hugh and his wife were living in Rhayader, Hugh now working as a slate quarryman. Son John was working as a shepherd in Llanyre just south of Rhayader, along with an older sister who was employed as a housemaid.

In 1902 Hugh Hughes died, and by 1911 Jane and her son John had moved down to Treharris in Glamorganshire, where John was employed as a coal haulier. Also in the same house was another daughter, Harriet, together with her husband. A record in the minute books of the Rhayader Poor Law Union, for the payment of non-resident relief, shows that Jane had been receiving four shillings a week from the Merthyr Union at this same address for the quarter ending 8 May 1907.

Pen-y-gwaith would eventually be abandoned. Some remains of the cottage can be seen today (*see pp. 170–171*).

59. Cwm-clyd

This was home to lead miner William Meredith, his wife Mary and their sons John and David, the latter working as a lead crusher. There were also two further sons:

Thomas, who was employed as a servant at Rhiwnant farm, and William Jnr, employed at Llanerch-y-cawr; and two daughters: Elizabeth Ann, who was a servant for the Baptist Minister, Seth Thomas, at Abernant, and Clara, a servant at Pant-y-blodau. All lived within the watershed area.

In 1895, son William married Elizabeth Jane Morgan who had been living close by at Llwyn-dale. Two years later, in 1897, Elizabeth Ann married Thomas Charles Griffiths from Abernant, and by 1901 they were running a grocer's shop in the Elan Village. Elizabeth's sister Clara was also employed there as a housemaid. Back at Cwm-clyd William was now a farm labourer. Son Thomas had returned home, and he and his brothers, David and John, were working as lead miners. William Jnr and his wife had gone to live in the parish of Upper Gwnnws in Cardiganshire, where William had found work as a shepherd. In 1904 Elizabeth Ann's husband died at the age of 42. Sons John and Thomas would go on to find work with the Corporation.

The Meredith family moved out in around 1905, and Cwm-clyd would soon be taken over by the Williams family from Dol-y-mynach. So, by 1911 daughter Elizabeth Ann (now a widow with four children) had gone to live in Builth Wells, and living with her was her father, William and brother Thomas, who were both employed as bricklayers. Son William had moved a short distance from Upper Gwnnws to Ysbyty Ystwyth in Cardiganshire where he was employed as a lead miner. David had married Edith Annie Evans in 1907 and the couple went on to run the Crown Inn in Rhayader. Sadly, David's wife died the following year, but in 1911 David was still running the Crown Inn, and living with him was his mother, Mary. Clara was working as a house-keeper for farmer David Price at Daverneithon in Nantmel; and John, having married Catherine Annie Pugh in 1910, was still employed by the Corporation and living at No. 3 Elan Village.

Later on, David was also employed by the Corporation, and Thomas moved to Birmingham, possibly as a result of him working for the Corporation.

60. Nant-y-Car

This farm was home to a widow, Ann Pugh and her two sons, Richard and David, together with grandson Robert Edward Sharp. They also employed Sarah Jane Roberts from T'yn-y-gors as a servant.

In April 1896 David married Emmeline Price from Gro-uchaf, and a month later David's mother Ann died (the address listed at her burial in Cwmdeuddwr was given as Merthyr Vale, late of Nant-y-Car). In 1900 Richard married Hannah Matilda Conway in Dolgellau. Also by this time, David had moved to Merthyr Cynog between Builth and Brecon.

By 1901 Richard was shepherding at Nant-y-Car, along with his new wife and his nephew Robert Edward Sharp, also working as a shepherd. David and Emmeline were still in Merthyr Cynog at a farm called Cwmcar where David was a shepherd.

TOP: Nant-y-Car farm (60) in 1892 (*by permission of the Library of Birmingham MS944 BCC ST 2008/214/Box 45*). BOTTOM: The ruins of Nant-y-Car (60) in 2015 (*note the group of trees still standing*)

Ruins of Bryn-Iago

TOP: Bryn-Iago (61) on the River Claerwen (*Lloyd Lewis Collection*)
BOTTOM: The ruins of Bryn-Iago (61) pictured in 2018

Richard continued at Nant-y-Car until at least 1902. The farm would never be flooded, even under the planned second phase; however, the family had to move out, and the farm was demolished and abandoned.

By 1911 Richard was farming near Machynlleth, and David was a shepherd in Garth near Builth, though he and his wife Emmeline would soon return home to farm at Ty-coch in the parish of Llanwrthwl. In 1911 Robert Edward Sharp was employed as a waggoner at Gwardolau farm near Cwmdeuddwr.

As has been noted, Nant-y-Car would never be flooded and one could argue that it should never have been taken down. It stood at an elevation of 960 feet (the top water level of the planned Dol-y-mynach reservoir was only 900 feet), and it would have been situated 650 yards from the end of the reservoir.

Remains of the property can still be seen today (*see also p. 172*).

61. Bryn-Iago

This was home to John Price (a carpenter in a lead mine), his wife Jane, and their son John Walter, who was working as a lead miner. By 1901 things were much the same, except that John was now working as a stonemason and his son as a carpenter. In 1903 another son, David Thomas, who had returned home, died at the age of 32. He had previously been employed as a shepherd at Llanfadog, just outside the watershed. The family remained at Bryn-Iago until about 1905.

Bryn-Iago would be lost to the building of the Cil-oerwynt dam (part of the second phase of the works), so the family would have to move out. The property was part of the scheme of the Houses of the Working Classes Act, so would need to be replaced by the Corporation. This was carried out by the building of a cottage adjacent to the old Cwm Elan Lead Mine. At the time of this decision, John was employed by the Corporation. However, it does not appear that John and his family ever occupied the new cottage, as by 1907 John was farming at Nant-yr-haidd near Cwmdeuddwr. John's wife died in 1907, and by 1911 Nant-yr-haidd was being farmed by John and his son. Later that year John Walter married Ruth Lewis of Glanelan and they would continue at Nant-yr-haidd for some years thereafter.

As already noted, the planned second phase of the works was much altered and the Cil-oerwynt dam was never built.

A few remains of Bryn-Iago can still be seen today (*see also p. 172*).

62. Cil-oerwynt

This was home to shepherd Evan Jones and his wife Margaret, their sons Thomas (a lead miner) and Evan, mother-in-law Mary Williams and niece Eliza Nora Williams. There was another son, John, working in the valley at nearby Dol-y-mynach as a farm servant.

In 1893 Mary Williams died, and by 1901 the family had moved a short distance to farm at the Cwm in Llanwrthwl. John had returned to live with the family and assist his father; Thomas was still lead mining and Evan Jnr was working as a shepherd at Bod-talog at the top of the Elan Valley (he would later work as a farm labourer at Blaencwm in Llanwrthwl). Niece Eliza Nora had moved away to work as a parlour maid in Lewisham, London.

In 1903 John married Eleanor Annie Rice, and by 1911 they were living at Rhosgoch farm in Newbridge-on-Wye. In 1908 son Evan married Bertha Lloyd, and by 1911 they were in Pontardawe, Glamorgan, where Evan was employed as a farm labourer. The following year Thomas married Mary Ann Lawrence and they also moved down to Glamorganshire, living in Maerdy where Thomas was a quarryman. At some point, Eliza Nora left London and moved to South Wales where she married Edmund Hughes, a colliery stoker in 1910, and by 1911 they were living in Treherbert. Later in life Eliza would return to live in Rhayader. At the time of the 1911 census, father Evan was living with his son in Newbridge, and mother Margaret was still living in Llanwrthwl.

The Jones family outside Cilewent (Cil-oerwynt) (62) in the 1890s. The picture shows (*left to right*): John Scott (visitor) Eliza Nora Williams, Evan Jones, Mary Williams, Margaret Jones and Thomas Jones. Note also the date, 1734, and letters on the door lintel (*by permission of the National Museum of Wales/ Amgeuddfa Genedlaethol Cymru REF: DF002489*)

After the Jones family left Cil-oerwynt, it became vacant and was uninhabited in 1901. The farm would have stood in the way of the planned Cil-oerwynt reservoir, but it was not taken down, and by 1911 the farm had been taken over by John Thomas Williams from Dol-y-mynach. As noted, the Cil-oerwynt dam was never built, and so the farm remained. In 1956 a new Cil-oerwynt farm was completed, and the old farm (which is of the traditional Welsh longhouse type) was taken down and rebuilt at the Welsh Folk Museum at St Fagan's near Cardiff, where it can seen today.

63. CERIG-CWPLAU

In 1891 this was occupied by a shepherding family who remained there all through the construction of the works: David Jones and his wife Elizabeth; their two shepherd sons, David and John; their daughters, Mary and Elizabeth, and a granddaughter, Elizabeth Ann.

All was much the same in 1901. Son David was now described as a general labourer (which may mean he was now employed on the works), and in 1895 daughter Mary had married William Morgans, a labourer from Blaen-Coel, and was living in Rhayader where her husband was now working as a milk seller.

In 1903 David Snr died; 1905 saw daughter Elizabeth marry shepherd George Morgan from Lluest-aber-caethon, and in 1910 John married the former schoolteacher from Nant-Gwyllt School, Alice Jones (née Abley).

In 1911, son David was farming at Cerig-cwplau, living there along with his mother Elizabeth and her granddaughter Elizabeth Ann. Mary and her husband William were now farming in St Harmon; Elizabeth and George were in the Elan Valley at Lluest-aber-caethon, and John was farming at Upper Llanfadog just outside the watershed.

Under the original plans, Cerig-cwplau would have been lost to the Cil-oerwynt reservoir, and because the property was occupied by shepherds it had to be replaced under the Houses of the Working Classes Act. Under this Act, a new cottage was built a little further up the valley, close to where the Nant-y-gader stream enters the Claerwen. However, with the changing of the plans and the original dams of the second phase never being built (being replaced instead by the Claerwen dam in 1952), Cerig-cwplau remained, but with a much changed outlook, with the Claerwen dam now as its backdrop. Interestingly, the replacement cottage (known as Esgair-y-gader cottage) was flooded by the Claerwen reservoir.

Cerig-cwplau still exists as a working farm today, the house having been rebuilt.

64. LLUEST-Y-GADER

A shepherd's cottage occupied by Abraham Davies, his stepdaughter Annie Evans and grandson Abraham Evans, along with a servant, William Jones Lawrence (who was also a shepherd).

ABOVE: Cerig-cwplau (63) in 1892 (*by the permission of the Library of Birmingham MS944 BCC ST 2008/214/ Box 45*). BELOW: Cerig-cwplau (63) in 2018, situated below the Claerwen dam. Although the house has been rebuilt, it is still possible to make out the original stone enclosure, especially from above

In 1900 Abraham Davies died. At the time he was living at Ty-bach, close to the site of the Caban-coch dam. By 1901 Annie and her son Abraham were living in one of the workmen's huts at Pen-y-gareg. She appears to have married Evan Jones from Machynlleth in 1895 (Evan was employed on the works as a crane driver). William Jones Lawrence was lodging with Benjamin Davies the tailor and his family at Llanfadog cottage, and was employed as a crane labourer.

Later in 1901 William Jones Lawrence married Eliza Davies, but by 1911 they had all left the area. Annie and her husband were in Gwaun-cae-Gurwen near Ammanford, where Evan was employed as a colliery blacksmith, and close by, in Cwmgorse, her son Abraham (now married to Lizzie) was employed as a colliery shunter. After some time in North Wales, William Jones Lawrence moved near to Neath in South Wales, where he was employed as a mine repairer.

Lluest-y-gader became unoccupied. It was well away from the works but it would eventually become abandoned.

65. NANT-Y-BEDDAU

This was home to sheep farmer Evan Price and his three sons, Daniel, John and Evan, and their housekeeper, Hannah Morris.

Nant-y-beddau would be untouched by the works, and members of the Price family would continue at the farm right through the time of construction and beyond.

In 1895, Evan Price Jnr, who was now employed on the works as a chainman, married Elizabeth Morgan in Nantmel. In 1896 he made an application to the Corporation, to allow him to bring materials over the suspension bridge and through the Elan Village, so that the property known as Ysgubor Fach could be renovated and made into a habitable dwelling. This property adjoined the back of the village and was owned by Robert Lewis Lloyd. The application appears to have been granted – but there is no evidence that Evan succeeded with a further application, this one to have a shop in the village.

In 1900 John Price married Mary Jones from the Henfron, and thus by 1901 at Nant-y-beddau were Evan Price and his son John (both shepherds), along with John's wife and Hannah Morris the housekeeper. Daniel was lodging at Llwyn-dale in the Rhiwnant valley and working as a shepherd, while Evan was living close to the Elan Village in what seems to have been the house he had restored, and was employed as a civil engineer's chainman.

In February 1902, father Evan died. A newspaper article records that his coffin was carried over the hills in deep snow. The coffin party left Nant-y-beddau in the morning, and it was dark when Evan was finally laid to rest at the Penuel Chapel in Llanwrthwl. The following year housekeeper Hannah Morris died. In 1911 Nant-y-beddau was being run by John Price (now listed as a grazier) and living with him was his daughter and two servants. John's wife was in the Brecon and Radnor Asylum in Talgarth, where she died in May of that year. Evan Jnr was still living close to the Elan Village, and continued to be employed by the Corporation, now as a painter's labourer. In 1911, Daniel was living at Blaen-Coel in the Elan Valley, and working as a shepherd. The following year he would marry, and he would eventually return to farm at Nant-y-beddau. When Daniel died in 1928, more than 100 mounted mourners followed his coffin over the hills. Some had to turn back, but over 80 arrived at the church in Strata Florida, where he was laid to rest next to his mother.

66. Pant-y-beddau

Pant-y-beddau would also remain untouched by the construction works, and members of the Roberts family who lived there would remain throughout the time of construction and afterwards.

Living at Pant-y-beddau in 1891 were shepherd David Roberts, his three sons, David, John (also shepherds) and Evan, and his three daughters, Jane, Margaret and Elizabeth. They were a completely Welsh-speaking family.

By 1901 son David had married and moved with his wife to a farm called Troed-y-rhiw, just over the Cardiganshire border near Strata Florida, and would remain here in 1911 (though he would later return to Pant-y-beddau). David's sister Elizabeth was also at Troed-y-rhiw in 1901. Living at Pant-y-beddau in 1901 were David Roberts, his daughter Jane as housekeeper, and son Evan, a shepherd – and this would remain the case in 1911.

67. Claerwen

This was home to the Lewises, another all Welsh-speaking family. The farm and the Lewis family would be unaffected by the works, the family remaining at Claerwen for some years thereafter.

In 1891 Claerwen was home to shepherd Thomas and his wife Winifred, along with two sons, Edward and William (also shepherds), and two daughters, Margaretta and Winifred. By 1901 all remained the same, except for daughter Winifred, who had died during the great snow storm of 1895 at the age of 28. It had taken two attempts to get her coffin over the hills for burial at Strata Florida, where all the Lewis family from the Claerwen are buried.

In 1904 Thomas's wife Winifred died. In 1906 William married Annie Evans, and by 1911 they were farming at the Claerwen. Edward had moved across the Cardiganshire border to farm at Frongoch near Strata Florida, and living with him were his father Thomas and sister Margaretta.

It is interesting to note that listed in the introduction to the 1911 census for the area are the properties of Lluest-y-gader (64), Pant-y-blodau (45), Dalrhiw (55), Bryn-Iago (61), Nant-y-Car (60), Llwyn-dale (54), Pen-y-gwaith (58), Pen-rhiwlan (51), Pant-tawel (48), Gro-isaf (38) and Gro-uchaf (43), although not entered as being lived in or unoccupied.

A photograph of the gathering of farmers, shepherds and others at one of the last shearings at Nant-Gwyllt before it all disappeared under the water (*Betty Davies Collection*)

This is strange, as while some of these properties might well have been still standing at the time, others would have been under the water.

Of the 298 people living in the two valleys just before the works began, over the next 20-year period (1891–1911), 73 had died, 45 had remained in the valley, with 29 of these in their original homes. A further 44 were in the parishes of Cwmdeuddwr and Llanwrthwl; 16 had gone to live in Rhayader, with 16 more in the surrounding villages. Within the rest of Wales, two had moved further afield in Radnorshire, 11 to Breconshire, seven to both Montgomeryshire and Carmarthenshire, five to Cardiganshire, and by far the largest number, 29, had moved to Glamorganshire.

Of the 17 people who went to live in England, five went to Somerset, two each to Warwickshire and Lancashire, and one each to Cheshire, Cornwall, Gloucestershire, Shropshire, London, Kent, Middlesex and Sussex. Three had made their way overseas, with one each in America, Canada and Australia.

There are 23 people whom it has not been possible to account for.

Of the 67 properties, 26 were submerged, with an additional 18 either demolished or abandoned. This left 23 houses, of which only 20 were in use, and 13 were occupied by the original families or their descendants. The church, chapel and school had been replaced, and the Corporation had also built six replacement cottages, only three of which housed original valley inhabitants.

What of the valleys themselves? As well as the six replacement cottages, Birmingham Corporation had made the temporary workers' village into a permanent workers' village, where 12 stone houses and cottages were built, along with a superintendent's house, office and school. Across the river opposite the village were the stables and the old Police Station houses which the Corporation had built, and these now also housed their workers. The old engineer's houses of Pen-y-gareg House, Pen-y-gareg Chambers and Tynewedd bungalow all remained but were unoccupied.

By 1911, then, the population of the two valleys was now 193 people. Of these, 90 were Birmingham Corporation workers and their families (except for the teachers at the school, who were employed by the County Council), with 72 of the 90 housed in the workers' village and the houses opposite on the other side of the river, and with the rest spread about the valleys. The majority of these people were incomers from England and Wales. Only four people from the valleys were employed by the Corporation – who, along with their families, accounted for 18 people, of whom four lived in the workers' village itself.

The two valleys remained a sheep farming community which included 13 farmers and 16 shepherds. As for the language of the valleys, the majority were now English-speaking with 101 speaking English, 77 speaking English and Welsh and only five people speaking Welsh only.

PART 6

What can be seen today

Detail of Terrier Plan "P", by surveyor Stephen Williams in 1893, showing the property Dol-folau, which would be lost to the upper part of the Caban-coch reservoir

6

B y using the map on p. 155 (*overleaf*) and the pictures in this section, together with the comparison pictures in Part Five, visitors to the area can find some of the ruined properties described in the previous section – either from the road or from easily accessible public footpaths, bridleways and byways. Of course, some of the ruins are dependent for their visibility on the level of the water in the reservoirs, and can only be seen when the water is very low, which doesn't happen that often. However, with the summer of 2018 being particularly dry and water levels low, many sites did emerge and these could be identified.

Exploring by Road

First of all, travelling by road and starting at Pont-ar-Elan just off the mountain road from Rhayader to Aberystwyth, follow the road around Craig-goch reservoir and shortly you will come to a large S-bend where the width of the road widens considerably. At first, you will turn away from the reservoir; but then, as you round the bend and face back towards the reservoir, straight across from you on the opposite side of the reservoir is Lluest-cwm-bach (2). This property was not abandoned initially, and continued to be the home of a shepherd for many years. It was later abandoned, and eventually restored

The ruins of Lluest-Torclawdd (1) in 2013

and converted to a walkers' bothy. Facing Lluest-cwm-bach across the water and nearer to you, where the stream enters the reservoir, the ruins of Lluest-Torclawdd (1) can be seen if the water is low. These ruins can usually be seen most summers.

Continuing your journey you will pass through the Hirnant farm (3) and on to the Craig-goch dam. There is parking on the other side of the dam, and this is the point where the Elan Valley Trail terminates.

Following on from here and now skirting the Pen-y-gareg reservoir, you soon round a couple of bends, and the island in the middle of the reservoir comes into view. Shortly after you will see a gateway, and from here you can see the ruins of Llanerch-lleyn (7) nestled in a few trees overlooking the island. This was never flooded but became abandoned.

The ruins of Llanerch-lleyn (7) just above the island in Pen-y-gareg reservoir in 2018

Once past Llanerch-lleyn you soon come to another large S-bend, and just after this, on the right-hand side, is a small car park next to the forest. From here you can walk down to the road and get a view looking up the length of the Pen-y-gareg reservoir, with the Craig-goch dam in the distance. From this viewpoint it is possible, if the water is very low, to see some of the walls of Ty-nant (8).

Travelling again along the road, in a short distance, you reach Pen-y-gareg dam. There is more parking here. If the water is low, take a look over the small humpback bridge, which is in the same position as the Pont Hyllfan crossing mentioned in the original journey in Part One. Note the deep rocky channel where the water is forced through; this was how the river was seen before the reservoirs came.

WHAT CAN BE SEEN TODAY
Showing properties lost or abandoned

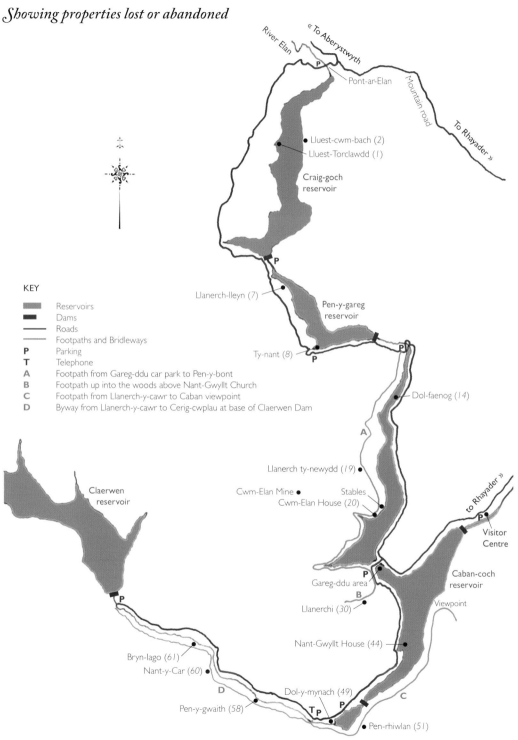

KEY

	Reservoirs
	Dams
	Roads
	Footpaths and Bridleways
P	Parking
T	Telephone
A	Footpath from Gareg-ddu car park to Pen-y-bont
B	Footpath up into the woods above Nant-Gwyllt Church
C	Footpath from Llanerch-y-cawr to Caban viewpoint
D	Byway from Llanerch-y-cawr to Cerig-cwplau at base of Claerwen Dam

River Elan

« To Aberystwyth

P

Pont-ar-Elan

Mountain road

To Rhayader »

Lluest-cwm-bach (2)
Lluest-Torclawdd (1)

Craig-goch reservoir

P

Llanerch-lleyn (7)

Pen-y-gareg reservoir

P

Ty-nant (8)

P

Dol-faenog (14)

A

Llanerch ty-newydd (19)

Cwm-Elan Mine
Cwm-Elan House (20)

Stables

to Rhayader »

P

Visitor Centre

Claerwen reservoir

Caban-coch reservoir

P

Gareg-ddu area

B

Llanerchi (30)

Viewpoint

Nant-Gwyllt House (44)

Bryn-lago (61)
Nant-y-Car (60)

D

Dol-y-mynach (49)

P

C

Pen-y-gwaith (58)

T P

Pen-rhiwlan (51)

The ruins of Ty-nant (8) taken in October 2018

Site of Dol-faenog

The site of Dol-faenog (14) taken in September 2018 when the area below Pen-y-gareg was extremely dry (*see also comparison pictures in Part Five*)

The flat area where Dol-faenog (14) would once have been, pictured in September 2018

The remains of Dol-faenog (14) as seen from the opposite side in September 2018
(*note the stepping-stones over the stream*)

Crossing over the bridge and continuing along the road, at the first bend, through the trees on your right, there are views down the valley to where Dol-faenog (14) would have stood.

Once around the bend in the road, and as the road straightens and is bordered by pine trees on your left, you will soon see a break in the bushes on your right-hand side, giving you a clear view down to the reservoir. If the water is low, a flat area with a few stones and evidence of walls and stepping-stones can be seen, which was once the property of Dol-faenog.

Continuing your journey you will soon come to the Gareg-ddu viaduct. Cross this and at the end of the viaduct is a car park just by the church. At times of very low water, looking down on the Caban side of the viaduct, the submerged dam comes into view. Also during low water levels, evidence comes into view of the properties that were lost here, including a few walls.

Remains of walls below the Gareg-ddu viaduct, pictured in September 2018

The road here now continues on to the Claerwen dam. On the way you will pass the small Dol-y-mynach reservoir. Just after this is an old building on the left-hand side of the road. This belonged to the farm of Dol-y-mynach (49), which stood just below this point. The house was taken down, but the area was never flooded, as the original reservoir plans were changed.

A little further on you will pass the telephone box at Llanerch-y-cawr (52), and then you will soon come to a large pull-in by a gateway on your left. If you walk just a few metres further on from here you will come to a gateway on your left where you can get a view across the Claerwen and see the ruins of Pen-y-gwaith (58). Now continue your journey. Further along the road, where the road and river make a right turn, the ruins of Nant-y-Car (60) can been seen on the far bank, situated in the bend of the river beyond a small meadow. At the next bend in the road, which goes left by the rocky waterfalls, you come to the farm of Cil-oerwynt (62), a modern replacement for the original farm which was dismantled in the 1950s and taken to St Fagan's Museum near Cardiff. Looking opposite the farm across the fields to the other side of the river you may just be able to make out the low ruins of Bryn-Iago (61). These last three properties can be quite hard to see from the road, especially in the summer when they can be hidden by the trees and bushes in full leaf. They are better viewed by walking along the old byway on the other side of the river (*Footpath Route D on map*).

The road continues and terminates at the Claerwen dam. Just below the dam is the farm of Cerig-cwplau (63), which, under the original plans, would have been flooded. From here you can retrace your journey to the Gareg-ddu viaduct, cross over the viaduct and turn right, bringing you back to the Visitor Centre and the Caban-coch dam.

Footpath Route A (*total distance: 6 miles*)

Park in the car park just at the end of the Gareg-ddu viaduct, by the church. Next to the entrance to the car park you will see a footpath. Follow this track, signposted for the Henfron, over the cattle grid, as it skirts around the reservoir. After about one mile you cross another cattle grid, and the track rounds a bend. Here, you will soon see, down to your right, a footpath sign leading you down towards the shore of the reservoir. Cross the stile and follow the path through the woods, taking care as the path winds its way over many exposed tree roots. There are good views of the Gareg-ddu viaduct from here. The path follows an inlet and crosses a boardwalk, taking you down to cross the Nant Methan stream. Once across the stream, follow the sign: you are now walking alongside some of the field boundary walls of the Cwm-Elan estate, probably created by Thomas Grove when he purchased the estate back in 1792. Continue on and you come to a stile on your left. Before you climb the stile, look over to you right, and just beyond the fence are the remains of a large wall with a small attached room. If you look closely at the wall there are chimney flues at each end: the terrier plans show this to have been a greenhouse.

From here, go over the stile and cross the corner of the field, before entering the woodland once again via a gate. Follow signs and in a short while you will see a broadleaved woodland information board. There is a small path which goes off to the left from here, and this will take you up to the ruins of the old Cwm-Elan Lead Mine (*NB if taking this detour, please take care, as old mine workings are dangerous*).

The back wall of one of the greenhouses belonging to Cwm-Elan (20) in 2013

The ruins of Llanerch-ty-newydd (19) in 2015

Some walls of the farm buildings of Cwm-Elan (20) can be seen on the opposite side of the reservoir, viewed from the Elan Valley Trail in 2018 (*see also comparison pictures in Part Five*)

Closer view of the remains of some of the Cwm-Elan farm buildings, taken in 2018

Photograph of Cwm-Elan House by W.H. Banks, with the rising water levels on the point of inundating the house (*image copyright © Hergest Trust Archive*)

Remains of Cwm-Elan
House and its outbuildings

Photograph taken during low water levels in September 2018
(*compare with the photograph on the previous spread, pp. 162–163*)

A view of all that remains of Cwm-Elan House (20), September 2018

For now, continue on the main path through the woodlands. The path soon veers left, narrows and starts climbing, passing over rocks and more exposed tree roots for a while before emerging out onto the hill via a small gate (this area can be quite muddy when wet). Continue up the hill. On your left-hand side, just before you reach a stretch of boardwalk, you will see the ruins of Llanerch-ty-newydd (19) on your left. This can be hidden by the trees in the summer, but during the winter and spring it is clearly visible.

Continue along the boardwalk, cross a stile and enter the next field. Take the path through the field, following signs and keeping the fence line on your left (ignore side gates) and emerge at the far end of the field by a metal gate. Go through this gate, cross the stream, and then follow the path heading for the house. This is the farm-house of T'yn-y-llidiart (15), which survived the flooding and is now a holiday cottage. Pass through its yard and you will come out on the other side, onto a trackway which will lead you all the way to the S-bend of the road by Penbont tearooms. From here, you can either retrace your steps, or you can continue on for a circular walk.

If continuing on, follow the road downhill, crossing the bridge below Pen-y-gareg dam. Look over the bridge: if the water is low you will see the deep, rocky gorge which the river flows through, again giving you an idea of what it was like before the dams came. Now continue along the road skirting the reservoir. Once again, if the water is low, keep an eye open along this stretch for the flat area where Dol-faenog used to be. At the end of a stone embankment topped by fir trees you will see a gate in front of you. Go through this gate and on to the Elan Valley Trail, which continues to skirt around the reservoir. When you enter the woodland part of the trail through an open gateway, if the water is low look out for breaks in the trees and look across to the other side of the reservoir. You should see some lengths of old stone walling close to the shore, which are the remains of the stables and farm buildings belonging to Cwm-Elan House (20); you may also see evidence of where the house stood.

Footpath Route B (*total distance: 1 mile*)

Leaving the Gareg-ddu car park, go past the church and you will come to a stream with a bridleway sign next to it. This is a steep but short walk of about half-a-mile up into the forest. It is rocky in places and can be wet. Climb the path and you will come to a wide forest roadway. Cross over this and continue straight on up. In a short while the path turns to the right. From this bend, in about 55 metres you will see a stream on your left. Continue on the path and in another 35 metres, just off the path to your left, you will see part of a wall up against a tree: this is one corner of the ruins of Llanerchi (30). There isn't much to see, and it is well-hidden amongst the trees and undergrowth. The path continues on to a gate, which leads out onto the hill and out of the forest. This walk can be made into a longer circular walk by taking the signposted path through the gate at the back of the car park. You will then approach the ruins from the opposite direction.

The moss-covered walls of the ruins of Llanerchi (30)

Footpath Route C (*total distance: 3 miles*)

Take the road that leads to the Claerwen reservoir. Along this road you will come to Llanerch-y-cawr parking area with its information board (on the opposite side of the road to a telephone kiosk). Park here, then cross over and take the roadway down past the telephone kiosk. You will soon cross the river by a metal bridge. Continue straight on where the tarmac road becomes a track, towards the old whitewashed farm of Llanerch-y-cawr (52). This is now a holiday cottage, and in front of the house is a board with some historical information. You will see the track splits here. Take the left-hand fork and continue along a rough track bordered by fields. At the end of the field the track enters some trees, crosses a stream and turns to the left. In a short while you will go through a gate and cross a ford. Take the left-hand (lower) track and head for the next gate. Go through the gate, then stop and look along the fence line on your right to a large tree with some large stones at its base.

These stones are all that remain of Pen-rhiwlan (51). Since the start of your walk, you have been walking in an area which, if the original plans for the second phase of dam building had been carried out, would all have been under water; and, as you look at the

All that remains of Pen-rhiwlan (51) pictured from the top of the fence-line in 2015

few stones of Pen-rhiwlan, this is the level the waters would have reached. Continuing now straight along the track, with views of Dol-y-mynach reservoir to your left, you approach some trees and lose sight of the reservoir. You will come to another gate: before going through this, take the short path down to your left to gain a closer look at the unfinished Dol-y-mynach dam. If it had been finished it would have reached a height of 101 feet, and stretched across the river for almost 950 feet.

Now, return to the main track and go through the gate (you are no longer under the proposed water level). Now the track begins to rise, and climbs all the way through another gate, eventually coming out just above the Nant-y-gro stream about a mile from your starting point. There is an ideally situated picnic table here, and great views over the Caban-coch reservoir. During your climb up the hill, if the water is very low you may have views looking down on the ruins of Nant-Gwyllt House (44); some of the old walled garden can be seen, a small stone bridge, evidence of other buildings – and, if lucky, you can make out the footprint of the house. However, it is quite rare for this to happen (the last time these were fully exposed was in around 2003). From here, retrace your steps back to the car. This walk is just over three miles there and back.

The photographs on this page were taken at various times during dry spells and reveal many, if not all, of Nant-Gwyllt's secrets

TOP: The ruins of Nant-Gwyllt (44), its garden walls and bridge clearly visible during a dry spell in 1984

ABOVE: A detail of the bridge over the Nant-Gwyllt stream, photographed during a dry spell

RIGHT: A view through a doorway in Nant-Gwyllt's garden walls, showing the low level of the reservoir in 1984

Labels on image: route of path · exposed walled garden · base of farm building

General view of Nant-Gwyllt's ruins from the walk in 2018 (*compare with 1893 plan below*)

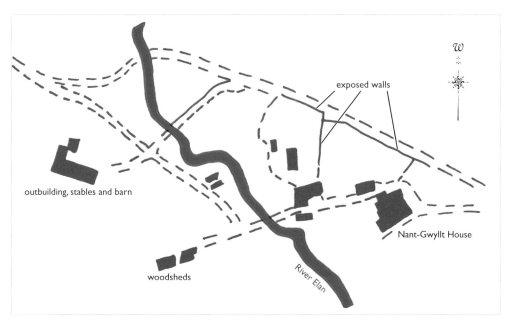

Labels on image: exposed walls · outbuilding, stables and barn · Nant-Gwyllt House · woodsheds · River Elan · W

A plan of Nant-Gwyllt as it was in 1893, showing other buildings behind the house, including a coach house, stables, kennels and greenhouses

Footpath Route D (*total distance: 5 miles*)

This walk starts from the same place as Footpath Route C. Park in the Llanerch-y-cawr car park, cross the road as before and head for the farm; but just before the first farm building, the tarmac road bears to the right and turns sharply back on itself. This lane, and the old byway which you will pick up, follows the exact route to Cerig-cwplau (63) as described in the original journey in Part One. Follow the tarmac lane all the way to the Rhiwnant farm (57), crossing the river of the same name just prior to reaching the farm. Go through the farmyard, bearing right and exiting the yard by a gate to pick up the old byway (which is a very rough, rocky and uneven track in places, and which can be very wet at times). The track climbs away from the farm and passes through three gates within a very short distance. Just after the third gate, you come to a junction where another track joins yours from the left. To the right of this junction you will see a flattish area with some large trees growing, and stones round their bases in places: these are the ruins of Pen-y-gwaith (58). Nearby on the right, just by a fenced-in area marked with a danger sign, there are some more building ruins. This area was littered with old mines, and Pen-y-gwaith was a miner's cottage. At this point you are quite high above the River Claerwen, and you can just about see and hear waterfalls immediately below you, and on the opposite side of the valley across the river you can see the old farm of Cwm-clyd (59).

The ruins of Pen-y-gwaith (58) in 2018

More evidence of structures around Pen-y-gwaith (58)

Continue along the main track and you will soon start to descend towards the river. As you are almost next to the river, you come to a gate. Go through this and follow the track around the bend in the river. A stream joins and follows the track for a short distance, and opposite here on your left are the ruins of Nant-y-Car (60). Why this property had to be cleared isn't known, as it would never have been flooded under any of the plans for the second phase. From here, continue along the rocky track climbing up to another gate. Go through this and you are now on a relatively straight piece of track, following the river and road on your right-hand side. Shortly, you will come to a point below which is the rocky cleft in the river where the Cil-oerwynt waterfalls are (these can be difficult to see from here, and are better viewed from the roadside). The track turns to the left here and rises, passing two rocky outcrops. After the second outcrop, straight across to your right is the modern Cil-oerwynt farm, and at the river's edge below you can be seen the ruins of Bryn-Iago (61), right by what looks like an island in the river directly opposite Cil-oerwynt (62). If the original plans had been completed, you would have been standing by the Cil-oerwynt dam, which would have been 109 feet high and 1052 feet long.

The track now continues all the way to the farm of Cerig-cwplau (63) at the base of the Claerwen dam – a farm which would also have been lost to the original plan (so, once again you would have been underwater here). From here, you can retrace your steps.

The ruins of Nant-y-Car (60) pictured in 2018, showing the track you have just come along
(see *also comparison pictures in Part Five*)

The ruins of Bryn-Iago (61) photographed in 2018, directly opposite Cil-oerwynt farm, which
is passed on the road to the Claerwen dam. Both of these properties would have been lost
to the original plans (see *also comparison pictures in Part Five*)

Alternatively, on the approach to Cerig-cwplau the track splits. The lower path fords across the River Arban (and you can do this if the water level permits), or you can take the higher track and cross via a small wooden bridge, making your way through Cerig-cwplau farm and down to the road below the dam. You can then follow the road back to your car, thus completing a circular walk of five miles.

There are other ruins dotted about the watershed, such as Lluest-aber-caethon (5), Lluest-calettwr (6), Cringwm (17), Ty'n-y-ffald (18), Blaen-Coel (25), Llwyn-dale (54), Dalrhiw (55) and Lluest-y-gader (64). These are more off the beaten track, and not so readily accessible from public footpaths.

As well as the ruins of the places that were lost to the reservoirs or abandoned, there are the farms which remained unaffected and still exist today. These have generally altered in appearance, having been renovated or rebuilt by the Corporation.

• • •

Table Notes for Appendix 1:

The bracketed surnames that appear in the family column show married names.

Where people have moved away from the area, the place name and the three-letter county code are given as follows.

BRE (Breconshire) CGN (Cardiganshire) CHS (Cheshire)
CMN (Carmarthenshire) CON (Cornwall) DEV (Devon)
GLA (Glamorgan) GLS (Gloucestershire) KEN (Kent)
LAN (Lancashire) MDX (Middlesex) MGY (Montgomeryshire)
OXF (Oxfordshire) PEM (Pembrokeshire) RAD (Radnorshire)
SAL (Shropshire) SOM (Somerset) SSX (Sussex)
WAR (Warwickshire) WOR (Worcestershire)

APPENDIX ONE: MOVEMENTS AT A GLANCE

For the area of research, the 1891 census recorded 287 people living in the two valleys. For the purposes of this study, visitors or the miners up at Nant-y-Carw lead mine have not been included, as these numbers fluctuated greatly, and consisted almost wholly of outsiders from Cardiganshire in the case of the mine workers. There were also three civil engineers employed by the Birmingham Corporation working in the valley at the time, and these have also been excluded. Stephen Williams, who was employed as an agent by the Birmingham Corporation, took a census in 1892 for the Corporation's own purposes. It was to be this census that the Birmingham Corporation would use as a starting point prior to commencement of work, with any settlements and claims referring back to this census. It was also used as information during the Birmingham Corporation Water Bill's progress through Parliament.

The population of the research area had increased between the time of the 1891 census and Stephen Williams' 1892 census, in which he recorded 333 people living in the valleys. Unfortunately, the Corporation's census only names the head of the household and the total number living in each of the properties. However, using both censuses it has been possible to account for 298 people living and working in the valleys at this time.

Just outside the area covered in this book, but within the watershed purchased by the Birmingham Corporation, and situated in the upper reaches of the Elan, are the farms of Bod-talog, Aber-Gwngu, Glan-Hirin and Aber-glan-Hirin, together with Llidiart-y-mynydd tenement. At the top of the Claerwen valley, where the Claerddu River branches off, there is also Claerddu farm. These properties together account for a further 29 people, making up Stephen Williams' total of 362 people living on the watershed. As these farms would not be interfered with, they are not included in this account.

PROPERTY: **Lluest-Torclawdd (1)**
OWNER/ VENDOR: **Edward and David Thomas**
OUTCOME: **Submerged**

FAMILY	FAMILY MEMBER LIVING AT *WORKING AS*		
	1891/ 1892	1901	1911
David Price	Lluest-Torclawdd *Shepherd*	Lluest-Torclawdd *Shepherd*	Rhayader *Labourer*
Elizabeth Price	Lluest-Torclawdd	Lluest-Torclawdd	Rhayader
Edward Price	Cwmdeuddwr *Farm Servant*	Lluest-Torclawdd *Labourer*	Treharris GLA *Farmer*
Elizabeth Jane Price	Allt-goch *Servant*	St Harmon RAD *Servant*	St Harmon RAD *Housekeeper*
David Price	Pen-y-gareg *Farm Servant*	Lluest-Torclawdd *Labourer*	Rhayader *Labourer*
Mary Ann Price	Troed-rhiw-drain *Servant*	Died 1896	–
Ellen Price (Davies)	Lluest-Torclawdd	Llangurig MGY *Housemaid*	Llanidloes MGY *Farm Contractor's wife*
John Price	Lluest-Torclawdd	Pen-y-gareg *Stoker*	Unknown
Evan Price	Lluest-Torclawdd	Lluest-Torclawdd *Labourer*	Died 1903
Annie Price (Price)	Lluest-Torclawdd *Servant*	Lluest-Torclawdd	Cwmdeuddwr *Waggoner's wife*
Lucy Jane Price (Morgan)	Lluest-Torclawdd	Lluest-Torclawdd	Treharris GLA *Coal Haulier's wife*

PROPERTY: **Lluest-cwm-bach (2)**
OWNER/ VENDOR: **William Edward Prickard**
OUTCOME: **Remained**

FAMILY	FAMILY MEMBER LIVING AT *WORKING AS*		
	1891/ 1892	1901	1911
Andrew Scott	Lluest-cwm-bach *Shepherd*	Lluest-cwm-bach *Shepherd*	Died 1903
Sarah Scott	Lluest-cwm-bach	Lluest-cwm-bach	Elan Village
John Scott	Lluest-cwm-bach	Lluest-cwm-bach *Stoker*	Lluest-cwm-bach *Shepherd*
George Scott	Lluest-cwm-bach	Cwmdeuddwr *Boarder*	Elan Village *Carpenter*

PROPERTY: Hirnant (3)
OWNER/ VENDOR: Edward Thomas
OUTCOME: **Remained**

FAMILY	FAMILY MEMBER LIVING AT		
	WORKING AS		
	1891/ 1892	1901	1911
John Thomas	Hirnant *Farmer*	Llanyre RAD *Farmer*	Died 1902
Anne Thomas	Hirnant	Llanyre RAD	Llanyre RAD
John Lewis Pugh	Hirnant *Shepherd*	Llanyre RAD *Shepherd*	Llanyre RAD *Farmer*

PROPERTY: Aber-Calettwr (4)
OWNER/ VENDOR: Edward Thomas
OUTCOME: **Submerged**

FAMILY	FAMILY MEMBER LIVING AT		
	WORKING AS		
	1891/ 1892	1901	1911
Thomas Rowlands	Aber-Calettwr *Farmer*	Beguildy RAD *Farmer*	Llanwrthwl *Farmer*
Sarah Rowlands	Aber-Calettwr	Beguildy RAD	Llanwrthwl *Housekeeper*

PROPERTY: Lluest-aber-caethon (5)
OWNER/ VENDOR: William Edward Prickard
OUTCOME: **Remained**

FAMILY	FAMILY MEMBER LIVING AT		
	WORKING AS		
	1891/ 1892	1901	1911
Mary Powell	Lluest-aber-caethon *Farmer*	Died 1899	–
John Robert Powell	Lluest-aber-caethon *Shepherd*	Cwmdeuddwr *Farmer*	Cwmdeuddwr *Farmer*
Mary Ann Powell	Lluest-aber-caethon	Cwmdeuddwr *Farmer*	Unknown
John Powell Owens	Lluest-aber-caethon	Lluest-calettwr *Shepherd*	Cwmdeuddwr *Farm Worker*
Andrew Price	Lluest-aber-caethon *Servant*	Unknown	Unknown

PROPERTY: Lluest-calettwr (6)
OWNER/VENDOR: William Edward Prickard
OUTCOME: Remained

| FAMILY | FAMILY MEMBER LIVING AT *WORKING AS* | | |
	1891/ 1892	1901	1911
–	Unoccupied	John Powell Owens *Shepherd*	Unoccupied

PROPERTY: Llanerch-lleyn (7)
OWNER/VENDOR: General Sladen
OUTCOME: Abandoned

| FAMILY | FAMILY MEMBER LIVING AT *WORKING AS* | | |
	1891/ 1892	1901	1911
Elizabeth Davies	Llanerch-lleyn *Farmer*	Died 1892	–
Henry Davies	Llanerch-lleyn *Farmer*	Llanerch-lleyn *Farmer*	Died 1910
Edward Davies	Llanerch-lleyn *Shepherd*	Died 1900	–
Mary Morgan (Davies) (Lewis)	Llanerch-lleyn *Servant*	Llanerch-lleyn *Farmer*	Abergwesyn BRE *Shepherd's wife*

PROPERTY: Ty-nant (8)
OWNER/VENDOR: General Sladen
OUTCOME: Submerged

| FAMILY | FAMILY MEMBER LIVING AT *WORKING AS* | | |
	1891/ 1892	1901	1911
David Morgan	Ty-nant *Farmer*	Ty-nant *Farmer*	Died 1902
Anne Morgan	Ty-nant	Died 1899	–
Edward Morgan	Ty-nant *Farmer*	Ty-nant *Farmer*	Nantmel RAD *Farmer*
Elizabeth Ann Morgan (Griffiths)	Ty-nant	Ty-nant	Newbridge-on-Wye RAD *Labourer's wife*

PROPERTY: **Troed-rhiw-drain (9)**
OWNER/ VENDOR: **General Sladen**
OUTCOME: **Remained**

FAMILY	FAMILY MEMBER LIVING AT *WORKING AS*		
	1891/ 1892	1901	1911
David Williams	Troed-rhiw-drain *Farmer*	Troed-rhiw-drain *Farmer*	Died
Mary Williams	Troed-rhiw-drain	Troed-rhiw-drain	Died
Mary Williams	Troed-rhiw-drain	Died 1892	–
David Williams	Troed-rhiw-drain *Farmer*	Troed-rhiw-drain *Farmer*	Troed-rhiw-drain *Farmer*
William Walter Williams	Troed-rhiw-drain	Troed-rhiw-drain	Troed-rhiw-drain *Shepherd*

PROPERTY: **Allt-goch-fach (10)**
OWNER/ VENDOR: **General Sladen**
OUTCOME: **Submerged**

FAMILY	FAMILY MEMBER LIVING AT *WORKING AS*		
	1891/ 1892	1901	1911
–	Unoccupied	workers/ shop	–

PROPERTY: **Allt-goch (11)**
OWNER/ VENDOR: **General Sladen**
OUTCOME: **Remained**

FAMILY	FAMILY MEMBER LIVING AT *WORKING AS*		
	1891/ 1892	1901	1911
Sarah Hughes	Allt-goch *Farmer*	Allt-goch *Farmer*	Died 1903
William Hughes	Allt-goch *Farmer*	Allt-goch *Farmer*	Llanwrthwl *Farmer*
John Hughes	Allt-goch *Farmer*	Allt-goch *Farmer*	Llanwrthwl *Farmer*

PROPERTY: Pen-y-gareg (12)
OWNER/VENDOR: General Sladen
OUTCOME: Remained

FAMILY	FAMILY MEMBER LIVING AT *WORKING AS*		
	1891/1892	1901	1911
David Evans	Pen-y-gareg *Farmer*	Pen-y-gareg *Farmer*	Pen-y-gareg *Farmer*
Anne Evans	Pen-y-gareg *Housekeeper*	Pen-y-gareg *Housekeeper*	Pen-y-gareg *Housekeeper*
Mary Anne Evans	Pen-y-gareg *Servant*	Unknown	Unknown

PROPERTY: Pen-y-bont (13)
OWNER/VENDOR: General Sladen
OUTCOME: Remained

FAMILY	FAMILY MEMBER LIVING AT *WORKING AS*		
	1891/1892	1901	1911
–	Unoccupied	workers	Unoccupied

PROPERTY: Dol-faenog (14)
OWNER/VENDOR: Edward Thomas Evans
OUTCOME: Submerged

FAMILY	FAMILY MEMBER LIVING AT *WORKING AS*		
	1891/1892	1901	1911
Edward Evans	Dol-faenog *Shepherd*	Dol-faenog *Farmer*	Died 1904
Martha Evans	Dol-faenog	Dol-faenog	Died 1907
Mary Anne Evans (Evans)	Dol-faenog	Dol-faenog	Allt-goch *Farmer's wife*
Edward James Evans	Dol-faenog	Dol-faenog *Shepherd*	Mountain Ash GLA *Miner*

PROPERTY: Ty'n-y-llidiart (15)
OWNER/VENDOR: **William Edward Prickard**
OUTCOME: **Remained**

FAMILY	FAMILY MEMBER LIVING AT *WORKING AS*		
	1891/1892	1901	1911
William Ingram	Ty'n-y-llidiart *Farmer*	Ty'n-y-llidiart *Farmer*	Ty'n-y-llidiart *Retired*
Jane Ingram	Ty'n-y-llidiart	Ty'n-y-llidiart	Ty'n-y-llidiart

PROPERTY: Dol-folau (16)
OWNER/VENDOR: **Robert Lewis Lloyd**
OUTCOME: **Submerged**

FAMILY	FAMILY MEMBER LIVING AT *WORKING AS*		
	1891/1892	1901	1911
Thomas Morgans	Dol-folau *Farmer*	Dol-folau *Farmer*	Llangurig MGY *Farmer*
Mary Morgans	Dol-folau	Died 1894	–
Mary Ann Morgans (Davies)	Ty-nant *Visitor*	Pen-y-bont *Labourer's wife*	Merthyr Tydfil GLA *Colliery Fireman's wife*
Thomas Richard Morgans	Dol-folau	Bewdley WOR *Chainman*	Penybont Station RAD *Walksman*
Evan Price Morgans	Dol-folau	Dol-folau *Agricultural Labourer*	Rhayader *Quarry Labourer*
Elizabeth Morgans (Norman)	Dol-folau	Aberedw RAD *Cook*	Talgarth BRE *Blacksmith's wife*
Eveline Morgans	Dol-folau	Dol-folau	Rhayader *Shopkeeper*
Edward Arthur Morgans	Dol-folau	Dol-folau *Agricultural Labourer*	Cwmdeuddwr *Farmer*
Richard Charles Morgans	Dol-folau	Dol-folau *Agricultural Labourer*	Mountain Ash GLA *Miner*
William Alfred Morgans	Dol-folau	Dol-folau *Agricultural Labourer*	Aber-gwngu *Farm Labourer*
David Ivor Morgans	Dol-folau	Dol-folau *Agricultural Labourer*	Llangurig MGY *Waggoner*

PROPERTY: Cringwm (17)
OWNER/ VENDOR: William Edward Prickard
OUTCOME: Abandoned

FAMILY	FAMILY MEMBER LIVING AT		
	WORKING AS		
	1891/ 1892	1901	1911
–	Unoccupied	Unoccupied	Unoccupied

PROPERTY: Ty'n-y-ffald (18)
OWNER/ VENDOR: William Edward Prickard
OUTCOME: Abandoned

FAMILY	FAMILY MEMBER LIVING AT		
	WORKING AS		
	1891/ 1892	1901	1911
–	Unoccupied	Workers	Unoccupied

PROPERTY: Llanerch-ty-newydd (19)
OWNER/ VENDOR: Robert Lewis Lloyd
OUTCOME: Abandoned

FAMILY	FAMILY MEMBER LIVING AT		
	WORKING AS		
	1891/ 1892	1901	1911
–	Unoccupied	Unoccupied	Unoccupied

PROPERTY: Cwm-Elan House (20)
OWNER/ VENDOR: Robert Lewis Lloyd
OUTCOME: Submerged

FAMILY	FAMILY MEMBER LIVING AT		
	WORKING AS		
	1891/ 1892	1901	1911
Edward Davies	Cwm-Elan *Gardener*	Died 1893	–
Fanny Davies	Cwm-Elan *Housekeeper*	Cwm-Elan *Housekeeper*	Died 1909
Fanny Davies	Cwm-Elan *Housekeeper*	Cwm-Elan *Housekeeper*	Rhayader *Boarding House Keeper*

PROPERTY: **Cwm-Elan Mine (21)**
OWNER/ VENDOR: **Robert Lewis Lloyd**
OUTCOME: **Abandoned**

FAMILY	FAMILY MEMBER LIVING AT *WORKING AS*		
	1891/ 1892	1901	1911
–	Unoccupied	Unoccupied	Unoccupied

PROPERTY: **Cwm-Elan Lodge (22)**
OWNER/ VENDOR: **Robert Lewis Lloyd**
OUTCOME: **Submerged**

FAMILY	FAMILY MEMBER LIVING AT *WORKING AS*		
	1891/ 1892	1901	1911
Anne Davies	Cwm-Elan Lodge	Cwmdeuddwr	Died 1901

PROPERTY: **Henfron (23)**
OWNER/ VENDOR: **Robert Lewis Lloyd**
OUTCOME: **Remained**

FAMILY	FAMILY MEMBER LIVING AT *WORKING AS*		
	1891/ 1892	1901	1911
John Jones	Henfron *Farmer*	Henfron *Farmer*	Henfron *Retired*
Margaret Jones	Henfron	Henfron	Died 1910
William Jones	Henfron	Henfron	Henfron *Farmer*
Sarah Jones (Williams)	Henfron	Troed-rhiw-drain *Housekeeper*	Troed-rhiw-drain *Farmer's wife*
Mary Jones (Price)	Henfron	Nant-y-beddau	Talgarth BRE Died 1911
James Jones	Henfron *Farm Servant*	Mountain Ash GLA *Miner*	Mountain Ash GLA *Repairer*

PROPERTY: **Cwm-Coel (24)**
OWNER/VENDOR: **Robert Lewis Lloyd**
OUTCOME: **Submerged**

FAMILY	FAMILY MEMBER LIVING AT *WORKING AS*		
	1891/1892	1901	1911
Rees Jones	Cwm-Coel *Farmer*	Cwm-Coel *Farmer*	Cwmdeuddwr *Farmer*
Anne Jones	Cwm-Coel	Cwm-Coel	Cwmdeuddwr
John Jones	Cwm-Coel	Cwm-Coel	Nantmel RAD *Farmer*
Mary Ann Jones (Bowen)	Cwm-Coel	Ashford MDX *Carpenter's wife*	Ashford MDX *Carpenter's wife*
Sarah Alice Jones (Boys)	Cwm-Coel	Cwm-Coel *Servant*	Washford SOM *Clerk's wife*
Ruth Jones (Edwards)	Cwm-Coel	Cwm-Coel *Servant*	Glyncorrwg GLA *Shepherd's wife*
Margaretta Jane Jones (Jones)	Cwm-Coel	Cwm-Coel *Servant*	Glyncorrwg GLA *Pumpman's wife*
Magdalene Flora Jones (Gilbert)	Cwm-Coel	Cwm-Coel *Dressmaker*	Glyncorrwg GLA *Engine Driver's wife*
Beatrice Jones	Cwm-Coel	Llanwrthwl *Housemaid*	Cwmdeuddwr *Dairymaid*
Thomas Lloyd Jones	Cwm-Coel	Cwm-Coel	Cwmdeuddwr *Farming*
Anne Jones	Cwm-Coel	Cwm-Coel	Nantmel RAD *Nursing child*
Thomas Hamer	Cwm-Coel *Cowman*	Unknown	Unknown

PROPERTY: **Blaen-Coel (25)**
OWNER/VENDOR: **Robert Lewis Lloyd**
OUTCOME: **Remained**

FAMILY	FAMILY MEMBER LIVING AT *WORKING AS*		
	1891/1892	1901	1911
William Roberts	Blaen-Coel *Lead Miner*	Llanwrthwl *Farmer*	Llanwrthwl *Farmer*
Margaret Roberts	Blaen-Coel	Llanwrthwl	Llanwrthwl
John Thomas Roberts	Blaen-Coel	Llanwrthwl *Farming*	Llanwrthwl *Farming*
Effie Anne Roberts	Blaen-Coel	Llanwrthwl	Llanwrthwl

PROPERTY: Baptist Chapel and cottage (26)
OWNER/ VENDOR: Chapel Trustees
OUTCOME: Submerged

FAMILY	FAMILY MEMBER LIVING AT *WORKING AS*		
	1891/ 1892	1901	1911
Christopher Price	Chapel Cottage	Died 1892	–

PROPERTY: Gareg-ddu (27)
OWNER/ VENDOR: Robert Lewis Lloyd
OUTCOME: Submerged

FAMILY	FAMILY MEMBER LIVING AT *WORKING AS*		
	1891/ 1892	1901	1911
Rees Price	Gareg-ddu *Farmer*	Died 1898	–
Mary Price	Gareg-ddu	Gareg-ddu	Rhayader, Died 1911
Edward Rees Price	Pen-y-gareg *Servant*	Pen-y-gwaith *Miner*	Llanwrthwl *Labourer*
David Price	Ty-nant *Servant*	Gareg-ddu *Coachman*	Treherbert GLA *Miner*
Thomas Price	Gareg-ddu	Gareg-ddu *Farmer*	Aberdare GLA *Mine Labourer*

PROPERTY: Shop-bach (28)
OWNER/ VENDOR: Robert Lewis Lloyd
OUTCOME: Demolished

FAMILY	FAMILY MEMBER LIVING AT *WORKING AS*		
	1891/ 1892	1901	1911
Anne Griffiths	Shop-bach	Shop-bach	Died 1907
Emmeline Griffiths (Morgan)	Shop-bach *Servant*	Llwyn-dale *Lead Miner's wife*	Llwynpia GLA *Stoker's wife*
David Griffiths	Ty'n-y-llidiart *Servant*	Shop-bach *Labourer*	Newbridge-on-Wye RAD *Estate Labourer*

PROPERTY: Pen-henbren (29)
OWNER/VENDOR: Robert Lewis Lloyd
OUTCOME: Demolished

| FAMILY | FAMILY MEMBER LIVING AT
WORKING AS | | |
	1891/1892	1901	1911
Evan Price	Pen-henbren *Farmer*	Died 1897	–
Margaret Price	Pen-henbren	Pen-henbren	Died 1901
Elizabeth Price (Roberts)	Pen-henbren	Pen-henbren *Engine Driver's wife*	Rhayader *Labourer's wife*
David Price	Pen-henbren	Died 1894	–
Thomas Jones	Pen-henbren *Carpenter*	Unknown	Unknown

PROPERTY: Llanerchi (30)
OWNER/VENDOR: Robert Lewis Lloyd
OUTCOME: Abandoned

| FAMILY | FAMILY MEMBER LIVING AT
WORKING AS | | |
	1891/1892	1901	1911
Thomas Davies	Llanerchi *Shepherd*	Llanerchi *Labourer*	Marchnant *Farmer*
Sarah Ann Davies	Llanerchi	Llanerchi	Died 1904
William Walter Davies	Pant-y-blodau *Servant*	Died 1897	–
Thomas Davies	Pant-y-blodau *Servant*	Garth BRE *Farm Bailiff*	Garth BRE *Council Labourer*
Mary Ann Davies (Davies)	Llanerchi	Llanerchi *Housekeeper*	Llanfadog Hut *Labourer's wife*
Evan Davies	Llanerchi	Rhiwnant *Cowman*	Marchnant *Shepherd*
John Pryce Davies	Llanerchi	Abergwesyn BRE *Waggoner*	Llanelli CMN *GWR Haulier*
David Davies	Llanerchi	Pant-y-blodau *Agricultural Labourer*	Birmingham WAR *Labourer*
Margaret Davies	Llanerchi	Died 1899	–
Albert Edward Davies	Llanerchi	Pant-y-blodau *Agricultural Labourer*	Birmingham WAR *Labourer*
Sarah Davies	Llanerchi	Llanerchi	Marchnant *Housekeeper*

PROPERTY: Glan-yr-afon (31)
OWNER/ VENDOR: Robert Lewis Lloyd
OUTCOME: Submerged

FAMILY	FAMILY MEMBER LIVING AT *WORKING AS*		
	1891/ 1892	1901	1911
Howell Lewis	Glan-yr-afon *Labourer*	Glan-yr-afon *Roadman*	Cwmdeuddwr *Retired*
Mary Lewis	Glan-yr-afon	Glan-yr-afon	Cwmdeuddwr
Howell Lewis	Allt-goch *Farm Servant*	Glan-yr-afon *Stone Labourer*	Abercynon GLA *Miner*
Elizabeth Lewis	Glan-yr-afon	Termynydd *Servant*	Unknown
Esther Lewis (Carpenter)	Glan-yr-afon	Glan-yr-afon	Chicago USA *Accountant's wife*

PROPERTY: Nant-Gwyllt School (32)
OWNER/ VENDOR: Robert Lewis Lloyd
OUTCOME: Submerged

FAMILY	FAMILY MEMBER LIVING AT *WORKING AS*		
	1891/ 1892	1901	1911
Elizabeth Abley (Baynham)	School *Teacher*	Boughrood RAD *Teacher*	Norton RAD *Teacher*
Alice Anne Abley (Jones) (Jones)	School *Teacher*	Upper Llanfadog *Farmer's wife*	Upper Llanfadog *Farmer's wife*

PROPERTY: Nant-Gwyllt Church (33)
OWNER/ VENDOR: Commissioners
OUTCOME: Submerged

PROPERTY: Ty-bach (34)
OWNER/ VENDOR: Robert Lewis Lloyd
OUTCOME: Submerged

FAMILY	FAMILY MEMBER LIVING AT *WORKING AS*		
	1891/ 1892	1901	1911
–	Unoccupied	Refreshment House	–

PROPERTY: Tan-y-foel (35)
OWNER/ VENDOR: Robert Lewis Lloyd
OUTCOME: Submerged

FAMILY	FAMILY MEMBER LIVING AT *WORKING AS*		
	1891/ 1892	1901	1911
Benjamin Davies	Tan-y-foel *Tailor*	Llanfadog Cottage *Tailor*	Died 1904
Elizabeth Davies	Tan-y-foel	Llanfadog Cottage	Llanfadog Cottage
Benjamin Davies	Tan-y-foel *Tailor*	Baptist Chapel House *Caretaker/ Tailor*	Llanfadog Bungalow *Tailor*
Margaret Evans (Roberts)	Tan-y-foel	Pen-rhiwlan *Navvy's wife*	Salford LAN *Labourer's wife*
Jonathan Evans	Tan-y-foel	Llanfadog Cottage *Blacksmith*	Abercynon GLA *Tramway man*
Sarah Ann Evans	Tan-y-foel	Unknown	Unknown
Elizabeth Evans	Tan-y-foel	Llanfadog Cottage *Servant*	Hoole CHS *Lady's Maid*
Margaret Evans	Tan-y-foel	Unknown	Unknown
Jane Evans	Tan-y-foel	Pen-rhiwlan	Manchester LAN *Servant*

PROPERTY: Abernant (36)
OWNER/ VENDOR: Robert Lewis Lloyd
OUTCOME: Submerged

FAMILY	FAMILY MEMBER LIVING AT *WORKING AS*		
	1891/ 1892	1901	1911
Seth Thomas	Abernant *Minister*	Died 1899	–
Mary Ann Thomas	Abernant	Died 1893	–

PROPERTY: Gro Mill (37)
OWNER/ VENDOR: Robert Lewis Lloyd
OUTCOME: Submerged

FAMILY	FAMILY MEMBER LIVING AT *WORKING AS*		
	1891/ 1892	1901	1911
John Lloyd	Gro Mill *Carpenter*	Gro Mill *Farmer*	Rhayader *Retired*
Margaret Lloyd	Gro Mill	Died 1892	–
Thomas Lloyd	Gro Mill *Carpenter*	Gro Mill *Carpenter*	Rhayader *Carpenter*
Llewellyn Lloyd	Gro Mill *Farmer*	Gro Mill *Butcher*	Rhayader *Butcher*

PROPERTY: Gro-isaf (38)
OWNER/ VENDOR: Robert Lewis Lloyd
OUTCOME: Submerged

FAMILY	FAMILY MEMBER LIVING AT *WORKING AS*		
	1891/ 1892	1901	1911
David Jones	Gro-isaf *Carpenter*	Died 1899	–

PROPERTY: Gro-bach (39)
OWNER/ VENDOR: Robert Lewis Lloyd
OUTCOME: Submerged

FAMILY	FAMILY MEMBER LIVING AT *WORKING AS*		
	1891/ 1892	1901	1911
Ann Morgans	Gro-bach	Died 1898	–
Sybil Morgans (Rees)	Gro-bach *Dressmaker*	Llanfihangel Brynpabau BRE *Shepherd's wife*	Died 1906
Selina Beatrice Jones	Gro-bach	Llanwrthwl	Elan Village *Servant*
Evan Thomas	Gro-bach	Abergwesyn BRE *Waggoner*	Abergwesyn BRE *Waggoner*

PROPERTY: **Nant-Gwyllt Cottage, No. 1 (40)**
OWNER/VENDOR: **Robert Lewis Lloyd**
OUTCOME: **Submerged**

FAMILY	FAMILY MEMBER LIVING AT		
	WORKING AS		
	1891/ 1892	1901	1911
David Vaughan	Cottage *Gardener*	Bryntirion, Rhayader *Gardener*	Bryntirion, Rhayader *Gardener*
Walter Norbury	Cottage *Coachman*	Died 1895	–

PROPERTY: **Nant-Gwyllt Cottage, No. 2 (41)**
OWNER/VENDOR: **Robert Lewis Lloyd**
OUTCOME: **Submerged**

FAMILY	FAMILY MEMBER LIVING AT		
	WORKING AS		
	1891/ 1892	1901	1911
Anne Conway	Cottage	Dalrhiw	Died 1907
George Conway	Cottage *Lead Miner*	Died 1897	–
Edward Conway	Cottage *Copper Miner*	Dalrhiw *Lead Miner*	T'yn-y-gors *Former Miner*
Samuel Conway	Cottage *Lead Miner*	Cwmdeuddwr *Publican*	Cwmdeuddwr *Publican*
Benjamin Conway	Cottage *Lead Miner*	Dalrhiw *Lead Miner*	Llanyre RAD, Died 1911
Hettie Conway (Jones)	Cottage	Dalrhiw	Llanyre RAD *Farmer's wife*

PROPERTY: **Nant-Gwyllt Lodge (42)**
OWNER/VENDOR: **Robert Lewis Lloyd**
OUTCOME: **Submerged**

FAMILY	FAMILY MEMBER LIVING AT		
	WORKING AS		
	1891/ 1892	1901	1911
Edward Lloyd	Lodge *Gamekeeper*	Cwmdeuddwr *Gamekeeper*	Cwmdeuddwr *Gamekeeper*
Mary Lloyd	Lodge	Cwmdeuddwr	Cwmdeuddwr
Edward Lloyd	Lodge *Gamekeeper*	Claerwen *Gamekeeper*	Cwmdeuddwr *Labourer*
Catherine Lloyd (Price)	Cwm-Elan House *Servant*	Aberedw RAD *Housemaid*	Aberedw RAD *Road Repairer's wife*

PROPERTY: Nant-Gwyllt Lodge (42) *CONT.*
OWNER/ VENDOR: **Robert Lewis Lloyd**
OUTCOME: **Submerged**

FAMILY	FAMILY MEMBER LIVING AT *WORKING AS*		
	1891/ 1892	1901	1911
Alfred William Lloyd	Lodge	Bewdley WOR *Coachman*	Rhayader *Coachman*
Thomas Lloyd	Lodge	Cwmdeuddwr *Labourer*	Unknown
Arthur Henry Lloyd	Lodge	Cwmdeuddwr	Rhayader *Chauffeur*

PROPERTY: **Gro-uchaf** (43)
OWNER/ VENDOR: **Robert Lewis Lloyd**
OUTCOME: **Submerged**

FAMILY	FAMILY MEMBER LIVING AT *WORKING AS*		
	1891/ 1892	1901	1911
Thomas Price	Gro-uchaf *Farmer*	Llanwrthwl *visiting*	Llanwrthwl
Selina Price	Gro-uchaf	Gro Hut *Housekeeper*	Llanwrthwl
Emmeline Price (Pugh)	Gro-uchaf	Merthyr Cynog BRE *Shepherd's wife*	Garth BRE *Shepherd's wife*
William Dyke Price	Gro-uchaf	Cwmdeuddwr *Stone Driller*	Cwmdeuddwr *Farmer*
Agnes Price (Johns)	Gro-uchaf	Nantmel RAD *Dressmaker*	Constantine CON *Blacksmith's wife*
Martha Price (Jones)	Gro-uchaf	Aberedw RAD *Station Master's wife*	Aberedw RAD *Station Master's wife*
Thomas Powell Price	Gro-uchaf	Gro Hut	Llanwrthwl *Farmer*
Daniel Henry Edwards	Gro-uchaf	Elan Village *Grocer's Assistant*	Bargoed GLA *Fruit Merchant*
Thomas Alfred Edwin Edwards	Gro-uchaf	Llandrindod RAD *Apprentice Monumental Mason*	Unknown
William Hughes	Gro-uchaf *Farm servant*	Unknown	Unknown

FAMILY	FAMILY MEMBER LIVING AT *WORKING AS*		
	1891/1892	1901	1911
Robert Lewis Lloyd	Nant-Gwyllt House *Barrister*	Otterhead SOM/DEV *Barrister*	Bath SOM *Barrister*
Mary Ann Jane Lewis Lloyd	Nant-Gwyllt House	Otterhead SOM/DEV	Bath SOM
Robert Wharton Lewis Lloyd	Nant-Gwyllt House *Solicitor's Clerk*	Bryntirion, Rhayader	Died 1905
James Edward Lewis Lloyd	Nant-Gwyllt House	Army *Lieutenant*	Canada, Died 1911
Louisa Beatrice Lewis Lloyd	Nant-Gwyllt House	Kidderminster WOR	Machynlleth MGY
Mary Anne Jane Lewis Lloyd (Lewis)	Nant-Gwyllt House	Kidderminster WOR *Civil Engineer's wife*	Bromley KEN *Civil Engineer's wife*
Cecilia Joan Lewis Lloyd	Nant-Gwyllt House	Otterhead SOM/DEV	Bath SOM
Gertrude Constance Lewis Lloyd	Nant-Gwyllt House	Otterhead SOM/DEV	Bath SOM
Evan Roderick	Nant-Gwyllt House *Butler*	Llandeilo CMN *Hotel Keeper*	Llandeilo CMN *Hotel Keeper*
Eliza Anne Lloyd (Roderick)	Nant-Gwyllt House *Lady's Maid*	Llandeilo CMN *Hotel Keeper's wife*	Llandeilo CMN *Hotel Keeper's wife*
Laura Elinor Mitchell (Beard)	Nant-Gwyllt House *House Maid*	Gloucester GLS *Turner's wife*	Gloucester GLS *Turner's wife*
Alice Leighton	Nant-Gwyllt House *House Maid*	Tewksbury WOR *Cook*	London *Cook*
Jessie Tompkins	Nant-Gwyllt House *Laundry Maid*	Unknown	Unknown
Anne Davies	Nant-Gwyllt House *Kitchen Maid*	Unknown	Unknown
Thomas Richard Mills	Nant-Gwyllt House *Footman*	Llanelli CMN *Butler*	Llanelli CMN *Hotel Proprietor*
Pericia Hayes	Nant-Gwyllt House *Cook*	Unknown	Unknown

PROPERTY: **Pant-y-blodau (45)**
OWNER/ VENDOR: **Robert Lewis Lloyd**
OUTCOME: **Submerged**

FAMILY	FAMILY MEMBER LIVING AT *WORKING AS*		
	1891/ 1892	1901	1911
Evan Jones	Pant-y-blodau *Labourer*	Pant-y-blodau *Farmer*	Died 1907
Margaret Jones	Pant-y-blodau	Pant-y-blodau	Died 1902
Edward Evans	Pant-y-blodau *Labourer*	Pant-y-blodau *Agricultural Labourer*	Llanwrthwl *Farmer*

PROPERTY: **Pen-glan-Einon (46)**
OWNER/ VENDOR: **Robert Lewis Lloyd**
OUTCOME: **Remained**

FAMILY	FAMILY MEMBER LIVING AT *WORKING AS*		
	1891/ 1892	1901	1911
Evan Meredith	Pen-glan-Einon *Labourer*	Pen-glan-Einon *Farmer*	Pen-glan-Einon *Farmer & Postman*
Ann Meredith	Pen-glan-Einon	Pen-glan-Einon	Died 1910
Lizzie Meredith	Pen-glan-Einon	Unknown	Unknown
Naomi Meredith (Evans)	Pen-glan-Einon	Cwmdeuddwr *Labourer's wife*	Maesteg GLA *Coal Haulier's wife*
Ruth Gladys Meredith (Price)	Pen-glan-Einon	Aberdare GLA *Miner's wife*	Aberdare GLA *Mine Repairer's wife*
George Meredith	Pen-glan-Einon	Pen-glan-Einon	Died 1909
Teddy Hallybone	Pen-glan-Einon	Aberdare GLA *Lampman*	Mountain Ash GLA *Miner*
Margaret Hallybone (Morris)	Pen-glan-Einon	Pen-glan-Einon *Servant*	Mountain Ash GLA *Miner's wife*

PROPERTY: Pen-cae-haidd (47)
OWNER/VENDOR: Robert Lewis Lloyd
OUTCOME: Remained

FAMILY	FAMILY MEMBER LIVING AT *WORKING AS*		
	1891/ 1892	1901	1911
John Lawrence	Pen-cae-haidd *Waggoner*	Died 1898	–
John Lawrence	Pen-cae-haidd	Pen-cae-haidd	Pen-cae-haidd
Eliza Lawrence	Pen-cae-haidd *Housekeeper*	Pen-cae-haidd *Farmer*	Pen-cae-haidd *Grazier*
Margaret Lawrence	Pen-cae-haidd	Pen-cae-haidd	Pen-cae-haidd
Caroline Lawrence	Pen-cae-haidd	Pen-cae-haidd	Pen-cae-haidd
Jacob Lawrence	Pen-cae-haidd	Pen-cae-haidd	Pen-cae-haidd
Richard Lawrence	Pen-cae-haidd	Pen-cae-haidd	Pen-cae-haidd
Jane Lawrence	Ty-nant *Servant*	Allt-goch *Servant*	Cwm-clyd *Servant*
John Price	Pen-cae-haidd	Pen-cae-haidd *Assisting Head of family*	Pen-cae-haidd *Shepherd*

PROPERTY: Pant-tawel (48)
OWNER/VENDOR: Robert Lewis Lloyd
OUTCOME: Abandoned

FAMILY	FAMILY MEMBER LIVING AT *WORKING AS*		
	1891/ 1892	1901	1911
–	Unoccupied	*see Llwyn-dale (54)*	Unoccupied

PROPERTY: Dol-y-mynach (49)
OWNER/VENDOR: Robert Lewis Lloyd
OUTCOME: Demolished

FAMILY	FAMILY MEMBER LIVING AT *WORKING AS*		
	1891/ 1892	1901	1911
David Williams	Dol-y-mynach *Farmer*	Dol-y-mynach *Farmer*	Cwm-clyd *Farmer*
Jane Williams	Dol-y-mynach	Dol-y-mynach	Cwm-clyd
John Thomas Williams	Dol-y-mynach	Dol-y-mynach	Cil-oerwynt *Farmer*

PROPERTY: **Dol-y-mynach (49)** *CONT.*
OWNER/ VENDOR: **Robert Lewis Lloyd**
OUTCOME: **Demolished**

| FAMILY | FAMILY MEMBER LIVING AT | | |
| | *WORKING AS* | | |
	1891/ 1892	1901	1911
Catherine Williams (Jones)	Dol-y-mynach	Dol-y-mynach	Nantmel RAD *Farmer's wife*
David Alfred Williams	Dol-y-mynach	Dol-y-mynach	St Harmon RAD *Farmer*
Sarah Williams	Dol-y-mynach	Dol-y-mynach	St Harmon RAD *Housekeeper*
Benjamin Williams	Dol-y-mynach	Dol-y-mynach	Cwm-clyd *Farming*
Llewellyn Williams	Dol-y-mynach	Narberth PEM *Apprentice Cabinetmaker*	Cwm-clyd *Farming*

PROPERTY: **Marchnant (50)**
OWNER/ VENDOR: **Robert Lewis Lloyd**
OUTCOME: **Remained**

| FAMILY | FAMILY MEMBER LIVING AT | | |
| | *WORKING AS* | | |
	1891/ 1892	1901	1911
John Price	Marchnant *Shepherd*	Gro-uchaf *Shepherd*	Died 1909
Elizabeth Price	Marchnant	Gro-uchaf	Rhayader
Walter Price	Llanerch-y-cawr *Servant*	Aberdare GLA *Coal Miner*	Aberdare GLA *Mine Repairer*
Elizabeth Price (Rowlands)	Marchnant	Aberystwyth CGN *Hotel Servant*	Llanidloes MGY *Farmer's wife*
William Price	Marchnant	Gro-uchaf *Agricultural Labourer*	Died 1904
Richard Price	Marchnant	Gro-uchaf *Agricultural Labourer*	Died 1910
Gertrude Ann Price	Marchnant	Gro-uchaf	Cwmdeuddwr *Servant*

PROPERTY: **Pen-rhiwlan (51)**
OWNER/ VENDOR: **Robert Lewis Lloyd**
OUTCOME: **Abandoned**

FAMILY	FAMILY MEMBER LIVING AT *WORKING AS*		
	1891/ 1892	1901	1911
Thomas Davies	Pen-rhiwlan *Agricultural Labourer*	Workhouse	Died

PROPERTY: **Llanerch-y-cawr (52)**
OWNER/ VENDOR: **Robert Lewis Lloyd**
OUTCOME: **Remained**

FAMILY	FAMILY MEMBER LIVING AT *WORKING AS*		
	1891/ 1892	1901	1911
Evan Stephens	Llanerch-y-cawr *Farmer*	Llanerch-y-cawr *Farmer*	Died 1907
Ann Stephens	Llanerch-y-cawr	Llanerch-y-cawr	Died 1903
Thomas Charles Stephens	Llanerch-y-cawr	Rhayader *Carpenter's Labourer*	Llanidloes MGY *Innkeeper*
Elizabeth Stephens (Jones)	Llanerch-y-cawr	Aberdare GLA *Surveyor's wife*	Aberdare GLA *Surveyor's wife*
John William Stephens	Unknown	Llanerch-y-cawr *Farmer*	Llanerch-y-cawr *Farmer*
James Evan Stephens	Llanerch-y-cawr	Birmingham WAR *Omnibus Driver*	Aberdare GLA *Brake Driver*
Clara Ann Stephens (Evans)	Llanerch-y-cawr	Rhayader *Railway Labourer's wife*	Western Australia *Labourer's wife*
Margaretta Stephens (Boucher)	Llanerch-y-cawr	T'yn-y-gors *Engine Fitter's wife*	Died 1909
Winsor Martin Stephens	Llanerch-y-cawr	Rhayader	Abercynon GLA *Miner*
Elizabeth Lewis	Llanerch-y-cawr *Servant*	Unknown	Unknown
John Jones	Llanerch-y-cawr *Servant*	Died 1891	–

PROPERTY: T'yn-y-gors (53)
OWNER/ VENDOR: Robert Lewis Lloyd
OUTCOME: Remained

FAMILY	FAMILY MEMBER LIVING AT *WORKING AS*		
	1891/ 1892	1901	1911
Mary Roberts	T'yn-y-gors *Charwoman*	T'yn-y-gors	Died 1903
Bertha Roberts	T'yn-y-gors	T'yn-y-gors *Housemaid*	Unknown
Elizabeth Roberts (Morgan)	Cwmdeuddwr *Servant*	Cwmdeuddwr *Farmer's wife*	Cwmdeuddwr *Farmer's wife*
Sarah Jane Roberts (Gwilliam)	Nant-y-Car *Servant*	Eynsham OXF *Gas Stoker's wife*	Trealaw GLA *Pipe Jointer's wife*
John Roberts	Unknown	T'yn-y-gors *Labourer*	Unknown
Matthew Roberts	Abergwesyn BRE *Waggoner*	T'yn-y-gors *Labourer*	Died 1901

PROPERTY: Llwyn-dale (54)
OWNER/ VENDOR: Sir Joseph Bailey
OUTCOME: Abandoned

FAMILY	FAMILY MEMBER LIVING AT *WORKING AS*		
	1891/ 1892	1901	1911
John Jones	Llwyn-dale *Farmer*	Pant-tawel *Weaver*	Died 1901
Margaret Powell (Jones)	Llwyn-dale *Housekeeper*	Pant-tawel *Weaver's wife*	Died 1902

PROPERTY: Dalrhiw (55)
OWNER/ VENDOR: Robert Lewis Lloyd
OUTCOME: Abandoned

FAMILY	FAMILY MEMBER LIVING AT *WORKING AS*		
	1891/ 1892	1901	1911
Edward Conway	Dalrhiw *Copper Miner*	Died 1899	–
See Nant-Gwyllt 2 (41)	–	–	–

PROPERTY: Nant-y-Carw Mine (56)
OWNER/ VENDOR: Sir Joseph Bailey
OUTCOME: Abandoned

FAMILY	FAMILY MEMBER LIVING AT *WORKING AS*		
	1891/ 1892	1901	1911
–	*Lead Miners*	–	–

PROPERTY: Rhiwnant (57)
OWNER/ VENDOR: Edward David Thomas, Rhys Llewellyn-Williams
OUTCOME: Remained

FAMILY	FAMILY MEMBER LIVING AT *WORKING AS*		
	1891/ 1892	1901	1911
Isaac Davies	Rhiwnant *Farmer*	Rhiwnant *Farmer*	Rhiwnant, Died 1911 *Farmer*
Jane Davies	Rhiwnant	Rhiwnant	Rhiwnant
Mary Anna Davies (Lewis)	Rhiwnant	Rhiwnant	Rhiwnant *Farmer's wife*
Catherine Jane Davies (Cox)	Rhiwnant	Rhiwnant/ Otterhead *Housemaid*	Etchingham SSX *Hotelier's wife*
Sarah Ann Davies	Rhiwnant	Rhiwnant *Servant*	Died 1909
Ursula Winifred Davies	Rhiwnant	Rhiwnant *Servant*	Ford SAL *Parlour maid*
Evan David Davies	Rhiwnant	Rhiwnant	Rhiwnant *Farming*
Ann Bennett	Rhiwnant *Servant*	Unknown	Unknown

PROPERTY: Pen-y-gwaith (58)
OWNER/ VENDOR: Edward David Thomas, Rhys Llewellyn-Williams
OUTCOME: Abandoned

FAMILY	FAMILY MEMBER LIVING AT *WORKING AS*		
	1891/ 1892	1901	1911
Hugh Hughes	Pen-y-gwaith *Lead Miner*	Rhayader *Slate Quarryman*	Died 1902
Jane Hughes	Pen-y-gwaith	Rhayader	Treharris GLA
John Hughes	Pen-y-gwaith	Llanyre RAD *Shepherd*	Treharris GLA *Coal Haulier*

PROPERTY: Cwm-clyd (59)
OWNER/ VENDOR: **Robert Lewis Lloyd**
OUTCOME: **Remained**

FAMILY	FAMILY MEMBER LIVING AT *WORKING AS*		
	1891/ 1892	1901	1911
William Meredith	Cwm-clyd *Lead Miner*	Cwm-clyd *Farm Labourer*	Builth BRE *Bricklayer*
Mary Meredith	Cwm-clyd	Cwm-clyd	Rhayader
Thomas Meredith	Rhiwnant *Servant*	Cwm-clyd *Lead Miner*	Builth BRE *Bricklayer*
Elizabeth Ann Meredith (Griffiths)	Abernant *Servant*	Elan Village *Grocer's wife*	Builth BRE *Widow*
Clara Meredith	Pant-y-blodau *Servant*	Elan Village *Housemaid*	Nantmel RAD *Housekeeper*
David Meredith	Cwm-clyd *Lead Crusher*	Cwm-clyd *Lead Miner*	Rhayader *Innkeeper*
John Meredith	Cwm-clyd	Cwm-clyd *Lead Miner*	Elan Village *Labourer*
William Meredith	Llanerch-y-cawr *Servant*	Upper Gwnnws CGN *Shepherd*	Ysbyty Ystwyth CGN *Lead Miner*

PROPERTY: Nant-y-Car (60)
OWNER/ VENDOR: **Edward David Thomas, Rhys Llewellyn-Williams**
OUTCOME: **Demolished**

FAMILY	FAMILY MEMBER LIVING AT *WORKING AS*		
	1891/ 1892	1901	1911
Ann Pugh	Nant-y-Car *Farmer*	Died 1896	–
Richard Pugh	Nant-y-Car *Shepherd*	Nant-y-Car *Shepherd*	Machynlleth MGY *Farmer*
David Pugh	Nant-y-Car *Farming*	Merthyr Cynog BRE *Shepherd*	Garth BRE *Shepherd*
Robert Edward Sharp	Nant-y-Car	Nant-y-Car *Shepherd*	Cwmdeuddwr *Waggoner*

PROPERTY: **Bryn-Iago (61)**
OWNER/VENDOR: **Thomas Pugh Evans**
OUTCOME: **Abandoned**

FAMILY	FAMILY MEMBER LIVING AT *WORKING AS*		
	1891/1892	1901	1911
John Price	Bryn-Iago *Carpenter*	Bryn-Iago *Stonemason*	Cwmdeuddwr *Farmer*
Jane Price	Bryn-Iago	Bryn-Iago	Died 1907
John Walter Price	Bryn-Iago *Lead Miner*	Bryn-Iago *Carpenter*	Cwmdeuddwr *Farming*

PROPERTY: **Cil-oerwynt (62)**
OWNER/VENDOR: **Thomas Pugh Evans**
OUTCOME: **Remained**

FAMILY	FAMILY MEMBER LIVING AT *WORKING AS*		
	1891/1892	1901	1911
Evan Jones	Cil-oerwynt *Shepherd*	Llanwrthwl *Farmer*	Newbridge-on-Wye RAD *Waggoner*
Margaret Jones	Cil-oerwynt	Llanwrthwl	Llanwrthwl
John Jones	Dol-y-mynach *Servant*	Llanwrthwl *Farmer*	Newbridge-on-Wye RAD *Farmer*
Thomas Jones	Cil-oerwynt *Lead Miner*	Llanwrthwl *Lead Miner*	Pontardawe CMN *Quarryman*
Evan Jones	Cil-oerwynt	Bod-talog *Shepherd*	Maerdy GLA *Farm Labourer*
Mary Williams	Cil-oerwynt	Died 1893	–
Eliza Nora Williams (Hughes)	Cil-oerwynt	London *Parlour maid*	Treherbert GLA *Colliery Stoker's wife*

PROPERTY: Cerig-cwplau (63)
OWNER/ VENDOR: **Sir Joseph Bailey**
OUTCOME: **Remained**

FAMILY	FAMILY MEMBER LIVING AT *WORKING AS*		
	1891/ 1892	1901	1911
David Jones	Cerig-cwplau *Shepherd*	Cerig-cwplau *Shepherd*	Died 1903
Elizabeth Jones	Cerig-cwplau	Cerig-cwplau	Cerig-cwplau
John Jones	Cerig-cwplau *Shepherd*	Cerig-cwplau *Shepherd*	Upper Llanfadog *Farmer*
Elizabeth Jones (Morgan)	Rhayader *Dressmaker (visiting)*	Cerig-cwplau *Dressmaker*	Lluest-aber-caethon *Shepherd's wife*
Mary Jones (Morgans)	Cerig-cwplau	Rhayader *Milk Seller's wife*	St Harmon RAD *Farmer's wife*
David Jones	Cerig-cwplau *Shepherd*	Cerig-cwplau *Labourer*	Cerig-cwplau *Farmer*
Elizabeth Ann Jones	Cerig-cwplau	Cerig-cwplau	Cerig-cwplau

PROPERTY: Lluest-y-gader (64)
OWNER/ VENDOR: **William Edward Prickard**
OUTCOME: **Abandoned**

FAMILY	FAMILY MEMBER LIVING AT *WORKING AS*		
	1891/ 1892	1901	1911
Abraham Davies	Lluest-y-gader *Shepherd*	Died 1900	–
Annie Evans (Jones)	Lluest-y-gader *Housekeeper*	16 Pen-y-gareg *Crane Driver's wife*	Ammanford CMN *Colliery Blacksmith's wife*
Abraham Evans	Lluest-y-gader	16 Pen-y-gareg *Servant*	Ammanford CMN *Colliery Shunter*
William Jones Lawrence	Lluest-y-gader *Shepherd*	Llanfadog Cottage *Crane Labourer*	Neath GLA *Mine Repairer*

PROPERTY: Nant-y-beddau (65)
OWNER/ VENDOR: Robert Lewis Lloyd
OUTCOME: **Remained**

FAMILY	FAMILY MEMBER LIVING AT *WORKING AS*		
	1891/ 1892	1901	1911
Evan Price	Nant-y-beddau *Shepherd*	Nant-y-beddau *Shepherd*	Died 1902
Daniel Price	Nant-y-beddau	Llwyn-dale *Shepherd*	Blaen-Coel *Shepherd*
John Price	Nant-y-beddau	Nant-y-beddau *Shepherd*	Nant-y-beddau *Grazier*
Evan Price	Nant-y-beddau	Llanwrthwl *Chainman*	Llanwrthwl *Painter's Labourer*
Hannah Morris	Nant-y-beddau *Housekeeper*	Nant-y-beddau *Housekeeper*	Died 1903

PROPERTY: Pant-y-beddau (66)
OWNER/ VENDOR: Earl Lisburne
OUTCOME: **Remained**

FAMILY	FAMILY MEMBER LIVING AT *WORKING AS*		
	1891/ 1892	1901	1911
David Roberts	Pant-y-beddau *Shepherd*	Pant-y-beddau *Shepherd*	Pant-y-beddau *Shepherd*
Jane Roberts	Pant-y-beddau	Pant-y-beddau *Housekeeper*	Pant-y-beddau *Housekeeper*
David Roberts	Pant-y-beddau *Shepherd*	Strata Florida CGN *Farmer*	Strata Florida CGN *Farmer*
John Roberts	Pant-y-beddau *Shepherd*	Unknown	Unknown
Evan Roberts	Pant-y-beddau	Pant-y-beddau *Shepherd*	Pant-y-beddau *Shepherd*
Margaret Roberts	Pant-y-beddau	Unknown	Unknown
Elizabeth Roberts	Pant-y-beddau	Strata Florida CGN	Unknown

PROPERTY: **Claerwen Farm (67)**
OWNER/ VENDOR: **Robert Lewis Lloyd**
OUTCOME: **Remained**

FAMILY	FAMILY MEMBER LIVING AT *WORKING AS*		
	1891/ 1892	1901	1911
Thomas Lewis	Claerwen *Shepherd*	Claerwen *Shepherd*	Strata Florida CGN
Winifred Lewis	Claerwen	Claerwen	Died 1904
Edward Lewis	Claerwen *Shepherd*	Claerwen *Shepherd*	Strata Florida CGN *Farmer*
William Lewis	Claerwen *Shepherd*	Claerwen *Shepherd*	Claerwen *Farmer*
Margaretta Lewis	Claerwen	Claerwen	Strata Florida CGN
Winifred Lewis	Claerwen	Died 1895	–

BIBLIOGRAPHY & REFERENCES

Barclay, Thomas, *The Future Water Supply of Birmingham*, Cornish Brothers Ltd, (Birmingham 1892, 1898)

'Birmingham's New Water Supply', *The Engineer*, (22 July 1904), pp 77–79

Bradley, A.G., *Highways & Byways in South Wales*, MacMillan & Co. (London 1914), originally published 1903, pp 85–92

City of Birmingham Waterworks, (undated), printed by James Upton Ltd, Birmingham

C.K., *By Celtic Waters*, J. Davy & Sons Dryden Press (London 1894) reprint, Forgotten Books (2015), pp 114–144

Clarke, Elizabeth, *The Valley*, Faber & Faber (2012), originally published 1969

Completion of the Elan Supply Scheme, City of Birmingham Water Committee, 1961

Crow, A.T. & E.A., *Elan Valley Waterworks, Auction Catalogue of Contractors' Plant & Machinery*, Sunderland (1907)

Hughes, R. Elwyn, *Cwm Cul a Garw, notes on the communities of Elan & Claerwen* (2006)

Judge, C.W., *The Elan Valley Railway*, Oakwood Press (1997)

Lees, E. Antony, *City of Birmingham Water Department, Elan Supply, A Description of the Works*, Cornish Brothers Ltd, (Birmingham 1908)

McBride, E. Anne, *Elan*, Welsh Water (1987)

Metal Mines of the Elan Estate, (undated), Welsh Water/ Elan Trust

Morton, Rita, *The Building of the Elan Valley Dams*, (undated)

Price, Hetty, 'Cwmdeuddwr Memories', *Radnorshire Society Transactions*, Vol 18 (1948), pp 46–51

R.C.A.H.M., *An Inventory of the Ancient Monuments in Wales & Monmouthshire Part III Radnor, H.M. Stationery Office*, (London 1913) pp 105–106

Tickell, R. Eustace, *The Vale of Nantgwilt a Submerged Valley*, J.S. Virtue & Co., (London 1894), private reprint (1995)

Wright, Sid, *Up The Claerwen*, Cornish Brothers Ltd (Birmingham 1948)

AMGUEDDFA CYMRU NATIONAL MUSEUM WALES, CARDIFF:

DF002489, Jones family outside Cilewent (Photograph)

HISTORIC HANSARD, OFFICIAL REPORTS OF PARLIAMENTARY DEBATES: (WWW.PARLIAMENT.CO.UK)

Birmingham Corporation Water Bill, 8 March 1892, Series 4, Vol 2, 265–307
Birmingham Corporation Water Bill, 11 March 1892, Series 4, Vol 2, 608–627
Select Committee 1 April 1892, Series 4, Vol 3, 464–465
Birmingham Corporation Water Bill, Select Committee 4 April 1892, Series 4, Vol 3, 536–552
Birmingham Corporation Water Bill, 26 May 1892, Series 4, Vol 4, 1857–1883
Birmingham Corporation Water Bill, 31 May 1892, Series 4, Vol 5, 337–348

LIBRARY OF BIRMINGHAM, BIRMINGHAM, SEVERN TRENT RECORDS:

MS944/114, Severn Trent photo albums
MS944/2008/214/Box 45, BCC Severn Trent photo albums

POWYS COUNTY ARCHIVES, LLANDRINDOD WELLS, LEWIS LLOYD DOCUMENTS:

R/D/LEW/2/663	Birmingham Corporation Water Act 1892
R/D/LEW/2/649–652	Petitions 1892
R/D/LEW/2/653	Speeches 1892
R/D/LEW/2/654–659	Act Evidence 1892

POWYS COUNTY ARCHIVES, LLANDRINDOD WELLS, OTHER RECORDS:

R/DX/63/28	Elan Valley Terrier Maps and Plans
R/DX/47/C/13	Assessments of buildings 1897
R/D/CL/1/18–40	Various photographs
R/D/CL/1/31	Description of valley ('The Filling-Up Of Cwm Elan', *Cassell's Family Magazine*, Vol 19/3, (1893), pp 196–199)
R/X/148	Photographs (under construction)
R/X/241/1	Album of photographs of construction
R/QS/S/1073–1116	Electoral Rolls 1900–1918
R/G/C/8–9	Poor Law Records
B/DX/36/110,113,116,117	Pictures in Post Card album

POWYS COUNTY ARCHIVES, LLANDRINDOD WELLS, WELSH WATER AUTHORITY RECORDS:

R/D/WWA/1/8	Compensation agreements
R/D/WWA/1/15	Various documents
R/D/WWA/1/23/1	Surveyors notes on properties 1893–1897
R/D/WWA/1/35	Agreements for sale
R/D/WWA/1/39	Miscellaneous concerning Water Bill
R/D/WWA/1/43	Tenants agreements
R/D/WWA/1/45	Valuation and provisional agreements
R/D/WWA/1/48	Mining
R/D/WWA/1/49	Tithes and Income Tax 1893–1905
R/D/WWA/1/58/2	Lluest-Torclawdd
R/D/WWA/1/59/2–3	Plan of Works
R/D/WWA/1/120/97–107	Notices to quit
R/D/WWA/1/122	Tenancies
R/D/WWA/1/123	Houses of the Working Classes
R/D/WWA/1/125	Correspondence concerning replacement cottages
R/D/WWA/1/142–164	Petitions against Water Bill
R/D/WWA/1/200	List of claims
R/D/WWA/1/362–299	Tenancy agreements 1905–1933
R/D/WWA/1/420–447	Tenancy agreements 1904–1939
R/D/WWA/1/472–478	Notices to quit
R/D/WWA/1/645–652	Edward Wood – 21yr Leases
R/D/WWA/1/653	Matters dealt with by Edward Wood
R/D/WWA/1/819	List of burials
R/D/WWA/1/842–848	Replacement cottage plans
R/D/WWA/1/850	Memoranda concerning replacement cottages

OTHER SOURCES:

The General Register Office/ Findmypast, Births, Marriages & Deaths

Hergest Trust Archive, Hergest, Kington, Herefordshire:
    Construction photographs by William Hartland Banks of Kington

The National Archives, London/ Findmypast, 1891–1911 Census Returns

The National Library of Wales, Aberystwyth, Welsh Journals Online

The National Library of Wales, Aberystwyth, Welsh Newspapers Online

Ordnance Survey Maps of the 1890s [First Edition, 6" to the Mile]
    (Radnorshire sheets, XIV NW, XIV SW, XIV SE, XXI NE, XXI SE, XXI SW)

Ordnance Survey Maps of the 1900s [Second Edition, 6" to the Mile]
    (Radnorshire sheets, XIV NW, XIV SW, XIV SE, XXI NE, XXI SE, XXI SW)

Powys County Archives, Llandrindod Wells/ Findmypast, Radnorshire Parish Registers

INDEX OF PLACES

For the 67 properties covered by this research, the reference number for each property is given in square brackets. Also, where alternative spellings/ formations occur, these are given in brackets. The places with completely different spellings are marked with an *

INDEX OF PEOPLE

Where people have the same name, their property is included in brackets as an identifier.